Church Library

FREE TO
Soar

FREE TO Soar

DR. DAVID & JAN CONGO

Fleming H. Revell Company
Old Tappan, New Jersey

Library of Congress Cataloging-in-Publication Data
Congo, David.
Free to soar.
Bibliography: p.
1. Marriage—Religious aspects—Christianity.
2. Love—Religious aspects—Christianity.
I. Congo, Janet.   II. Title.
BV835.C634   1987   248.4   87-20476
ISBN 0-8007-1560-8

Copyright © 1987 by Dr. David and Jan Congo
Published by the Fleming H. Revell Company
Old Tappan, New Jersey 07675
Printed in the United States of America

To the outstanding couples
who have attended our
marriage seminars.
You have taught us so much.
We offer you
our love,
our thoughts,
and our thanks.

CONTENTS

PREFACE

We love being married to each other!
We love the challenge of it
the pain of it
the agony of it
and the exhilaration of it.
We are both capable of living alone.
Yes.
But what companionship, what fun
and
what accountability for growth
would be lacking in our lives.

Through personal struggle and introspection
we have learned
that only as we love Christ more
than we love each other
do we have enough love
to love each other with.

We have learned that soaring comes
as a result of valuing each other,
it's as if we are angels with only one wing
and
we soar only by embracing each other.[1]

It has become our passion to share
that the power of love
is so much stronger
than the love of power.

We pray that Christ's love
will infuse your life
and
revolutionize your marriage
as a result of reading this book.

DAVE AND JAN CONGO

FOREWORD

It has been my opportunity to know and work with some special individuals over the years. These are people whose lives are consistent with what they teach and say. Dave and Jan Congo are two of those people who reflect in their own marriage what they share in this unique and practical book. What they say in this volume has been needed for years, but many have been fearful of being so honest.

The topic of "who has the most power influence" in a marriage relationship is often a critical issue. Yet how many books ever honestly confront this and offer a biblical and practical solution? Very few! But Dave and Jan have come to grips with the issue practically and biblically. Their unique approach of contrasting the dependent, independent, and interdependent marital styles will grasp your interest and attention.

Not only are new insights shared but they are also done so in a way that readers will be able to apply them to their own marriages. You who wonder, "Where has the romance gone?" will find simple and realistic ways of building the intimacy and sexual expression back into your marriage. Dave and Jan are quite open with their suggestions, so be prepared! They tell it like it is (or could be!).

Applying the suggestions in this book can put a new smile on your face and your marriage!

H. NORMAN WRIGHT

ACKNOWLEDGMENTS

It is with deep gratitude and appreciation that we acknowledge the contributions of the following people to this manuscript:

H. Norman Wright, for his willingness to review the manuscript and write the foreword;

Joan Bay Klope, a treasured friend and gifted editor, for her sensitive and professional assistance;

The men and women in our individual support groups, who prayed for us and loved us through this "creation";

Our two precious children, Christopher and Amy, who lived with us while we were immersed in books, paper, and thoughts.

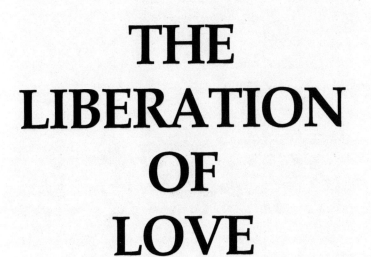

THE
LIBERATION
OF
LOVE

1

Confusion on the Marriage Front

FROM WEDDING TO WARFARE

Love may be blind, but marriage is a real eye-opener.

With a *whizz* the wedding ring flew forcefully past my ear. What on earth had just happened? Only a short time before I, Dave, was standing in front of forty couples, leading a marriage retreat. Now, a mere thirty minutes later, Jan's wedding ring was flying past me!

"I've had it. I can't stand being married!" hissed Jan. "This is no way for a human being to live. You've been doing your thing for years in our relationship and actually spiritualizing it. Now it's my turn."

What in the world has come over this woman? I wondered. It didn't take a college degree to see that Jan was angry— very angry. *Why, she's the perfect pastor's wife. She's beautiful and that certainly doesn't hurt. She's also intelligent, a college instructor, and always available—which is pretty convenient. What could possibly be wrong? Maybe it's just that time of the month. And besides, Jan has always been a little more expressive than me.*

What was wrong? Only the very foundation upon which we had built our relationship, that's all! The pain, hurt, and agony had been hidden from the outside world for years, and just like Mount Saint Helens, it was spewing forth.

But weren't we practicing Christians? Yes, and that was part of the problem. As a matter of fact, I was a pastor of youth and Christian education. That made Jan a pastor's wife. But Christians aren't supposed to have problems, are they? (We certainly can't find any scriptural basis for that statement!)

We were having problems and we needed to face them. Rage comes from feeling powerless, and Jan was certainly feeling that way.

Early in our marriage we received some very strong and convincing teaching about the marriage relationship. Both of us were committed Christians; we loved each other, and we wanted to make our marriage a great one according to God's standards. We were taught that in the biblical Christian relationship the husband serves God, and the wife serves her husband. Today we call this style of marriage the "unhealthy hierarchy." We also call it unbiblical.

At that time in our lives, however, we swallowed this teaching hook, line, and sinker. When living out this teaching, the husband is left free to do what he wants. Of course what he wants is God's will—right?

The wife is left free to be totally dedicated to the care and feeding of her husband's ego. She must become a revised standard version of her husband—his clone—if she is truly a submissive wife. Differences become intolerable and signal a rebellious attitude on the part of the wife. The wife's opinions and thoughts are not sought by her husband. All he wants is for his gal to be a rubber stamp for his preferences.

We attended a wedding during this past year, and the pastor addressed the young couple with these words: "You are to be involved in a partnership marriage." Then he turned to the groom and instructed: "You will be the head partner." Next he addressed the bride: "And you, my dear, will be the silent partner."

This teaching pressures a woman to hide a part of herself so she won't displease or upset her husband. It isn't long until she feels that she is inferior and inadequate, for her husband is the only one who has value in this relationship. Not only has she dropped her name to marry this guy but she has also lost her identity.

We know you've seen young women like this. They are radiant with hope and anticipation on their wedding day. Three years later there is a dullness in their eyes, a shyness and insecurity you never noticed before. They are lacking confidence, and often, love for the men they married. They don't want to be divorced but their need for their husbands is much greater than their love for them.

This unhealthy hierarchy feeds the egos of men with the enormous need to control. After all, a controlling husband gets to do whatever he wants. He is the only person fulfilled in this relationship. We call him a "married bachelor."

I hadn't really meant to become a married bachelor but that is what I had become. I was fresh out of seminary and wanted to prove myself in my first pastorate. I knew Jan would be a great asset to my goal. My responsibilities at the church kept me at the beck and call of people six nights a week, so I found my life revolving around my ministry. It is so easy when we are doing things for God to lose sight of this very same God.

There I was, leading a marriage seminar and expounding the chain of authority, and my wife, this asset to me, was coming unglued.

As a minister's wife, I, Jan, had spent a great deal of time studying the faces in our congregation. I liked the people but I didn't feel that they knew me. When I was with them I was the pastor's wife, Dave's clone. The only place where I felt people really knew me was at the college where I was teaching.

On that fateful day at the retreat, I stopped being a dependent woman whose entire life was built around Dave. Unfortunately I made the decision to build my life around myself and my career as a college instructor. With that resolution a two-headed monster was born and this monster would cause suffering for both of us. They say misery loves company, and we became the company of the miserable. We began to live out an isolate style of marriage.

Divorce was not an option for us. When we got married, we committed ourselves to each other for life. The decision then was not whether or not we'd stay together; we had to decide what kind of life we wanted to have together. How thankful we are now that we did commit ourselves for better or worse, because without that commitment we would have fled in the midst of the worst and never found out how good the better could be.

At that period in our marriage we lived in isolation from each other. Instead of Dave's being the center of my world, my career became central. Dave had been living that way since we were married, so the two-headed monster was alive—with all of the distance, loneliness, lack of sensitivity, power struggles, and unmet needs.

Eight years of challenge and choice passed. We were

both jostling to see who would be chief in our marital relationship. At that time Dave was the director of Student Services at a Canadian college and seminary. I taught at a university and played an active role in a Christian women's club.

One day Dave walked through our door and let it slam behind him in obvious frustration. "I can't take it anymore. It isn't enough to tell kids that if they're Christians things will just work out. That's not true! It's not going to help them face reality. I have to get further training— perhaps a doctorate in psychology and theology."

As amazing as it may seem, I had been waiting for those words for three years. Three years prior we had moved into our very first new home, built by Dave with the help of his dad and brothers. As I was praising the Lord for His goodness, a quiet sensation came over me and settled in that this home would finance Dave's education, when the time was right. It was as if I had been prepared to leave from Day One.

So Dave's words were greeted by an exclamation of joy. "Great! Have you thought about where you want to get your doctorate?" (Not a bad response from a woman with an overdeveloped nesting instinct who was caught up in her own career!)

It turned out that there were only two schools that offered the integration of psychology and theology that Dave wanted. Both were on the West Coast of the United States. Dave decided on the program that sounded as if it could offer the most to someone with his background. The application forms were completed, and we prayerfully sent them off, committing ourselves to go if Dave was accepted. The opportunity presented itself, and we headed off for southern California with a real sense of anticipation.

Christ's Hand in Our Crisis

It seemed as if we had the world by the tail. We absolutely fell in love with southern California. Dave was challenged by the program, our two-year-old son Christopher had made the adjustment easily, and we found a house in close proximity to the school. On top of that Biola University had hired me to teach. What more could we ask for?

Out of the blue my opportunity for teaching was put to an end by the U.S. Immigration Department, who ruled I could not teach and take a position intended for a U.S. citizen. Now we were faced with the financial reality of paying the school tuition, house payments, and food costs. During the first few years of our marriage my identity had come from being Dave's wife. Then I, in total frustration, had rejected that option and had chosen to base my identity on my career. This was going to be my vehicle to make a name for myself, and in the process find out who I was. Would I ever know who I really was? Was it an illusion to even ask the question?

There followed months of depression and agony in attempting to be a superwoman, just to prove to the world that I was worth something. Those months included silent moments of pain and fear when I wondered if indeed I was worth anything.

Paradoxically, this loss was not only my growing edge—it was also to become Dave's. In order to find healing, each of us is required to say good-bye to the old and hello to the new. It is true that we can refuse to budge, choosing instead to wallow in our grief and pain. But the result of those choices is this: we will break. There will be no flexibility and ultimately no love left in us.

Together we talked into the wee hours many mornings. We eventually came to see that we had been building our lives on "faulty foundations." We could have lived the rest of our lives spiritually and emotionally distant from one another, but we chose to face our pain and restructure the foundations upon which we were building our marriage. In the process we discovered that we were not alone!

2

The Misuse of Power

FROM MISERY TO MANIPULATION

What I love determines if I love.

John loves golf. In fact, just thinking about the game makes his blood race. There is nothing he enjoys more than being out on the green with his golfing partners.

He is an affluent businessman who provides well for his wife and children. In exchange, John demands total freedom to come and go as he pleases. His desire to golf is satisfied six, seven, even eight times a week, while his wife is allowed no childless moments. She is responsible for the kingdom of the home and her job never ends.

"Suzy is totally dedicated to the care and feeding of her husband's ego. Each day of Suzy's life is filled with plans: she plans food that Fred will enjoy, sex that will excite him, and conversation that will be stimulating to him. She plans a fulfilling life for Fred.

"She read somewhere that wives are supposed to submit to their husbands and she has been doing it ever since. The trouble is Suzy is rapidly losing her personality, her friends, and her cool. Her conversation is loaded with 'Fred says,' and 'Fred thinks.' Suzy has stopped thinking. She has also stopped going to church because Fred thought she was becoming too religious. She watches only the TV programs Fred likes and she has stopped seeing any friends Fred does not care for. She has for all practical purposes stopped living!"[1]

Bill is an anointed man of God. He studies the Word, prays, and teaches. With his wife and children in tow, he heads off to at least three Bible studies each week. Bill is so consumed with his studies, however, that he has no energy left for work.

He sends his wife out to bring in the bacon while he concocts grandiose plans for a worldwide ministry, studies his Bible, watches TV preachers, and catches up on his rest. When his wife returns home after a tiring day at work, she must face all the home responsibilities that await her. When she finally falls asleep at night, she is often awakened three or four hours later by an amorous lover.

All of these couples would affirm that they have a Christian marriage and yes, certainly, they love their spouses. But do they really? Needy love clings, stifles, manipulates, possesses, and controls. Needy love asks, "What can you do for me?" Healthy love affirms, gives freedom to grow, and supports the recipient of love. The healthy lover asks, "What can I do for both of us?" We get in such trouble when we confuse needy love with healthy love.

Although *I* should be a part of *we,* many suffer from a love that excludes themselves. The danger is, as each of these examples demonstrates, people can get stuck on *I* or on *you.* In order for *we* to even be a possibility, it is your task to connect yourself with the ultimate love Source, Jesus Christ, so you will have His available love. When this results, you will give your loved one that gift of a whole person. If you don't respect yourself, it is not possible for you to respect or respond to your partner's love.

An individual who feels unimportant and unfulfilled may choose to make unreasonable demands on his/her marriage partner. But it is not their job to make their spouse grow; it is their job to be in touch with the Source of growth and then experience personal growth.

Psychologist Rudolph Driekers discovered that behaviors chosen by partners with low feelings of self-esteem are generally directed toward these activities: excusing themselves for shortcomings, attracting attention, gaining power, and vengeance.[2]

Often, woman doesn't recognize a man's underlying feelings of low self-esteem and falls in love with what appears to be a "strong" man's confidence. Unfortunately, underneath his self-assured grin is a very insecure person. How he loves to grasp onto the teaching of husband as "head." Because of his insecurities headship is equated with power. At this point in time a married bachelor is created, not out of the dust of the ground but out of a few biblical verses taken out of context.

Our American society, with its emphasis on exploitation and competition, affirms to the insecure husband that being the head means holding all the power. He is rewarded for the very beliefs that will isolate him from his marriage partner and pit him against her.

The Married Bachelor: I'm the Head!

Headship becomes equated with power, and even though he may be a judge, the president of the bank, or a pastor, the married bachelor will overpower and dominate his wife to feel in complete control.

Because of incomplete and unfortunate teaching, many Christian women believe the Bible teaches that husbands are supposed to control their wives, and wives are to obey their husbands in all things. This teaching blinds women to the reality that overcontrol is a statement of the husband's personal needs.

One man would invariably order his wife to hang up the phone anytime he entered the room. He wouldn't let her spend time with her friends and banned her family from ever entering "his" house.

Another married bachelor sat in Dave's presence one day and informed him that if his wife would just submit, everything would be fine. To make his point he slammed his King James Bible down on Dave's desk. He and his wife had separated due to his constant physical abuse and his involvement with someone else. Now he felt it was of the Lord for them to be reconciled.

With that in mind, he had invited his wife over the evening before the session. After a lovely candlelight dinner, he presented his plan of reconciliation. She was lukewarm about the idea, and an argument followed. As their words became more and more heated, she fled from the house, only to have him follow her and push her to the ground with such force that her neck was bruised. She finally escaped after some struggle.

There was no remorse in his tone or body language. He quite simply believed that if she would just submit their problems would cease.

An insecure, domineering man doesn't treat his spouse as well as he would a neighbor borrowing a musical tape. And even though this is a masculine stereotype, we meet these men with increasing frequency in our marriage seminars and counseling sessions. A married bachelor is a powerful, competitive man who suffers from crippling insecurity, immaturity, and self-doubt. A real man must be tough, he believes, never showing weakness or anxiety. His every word is law; a scriptural mandate.

*In order for we
to even be a possibility,
it is your task
to connect yourself
with the ultimate love Source,
Jesus Christ.*

A woman is a weak and inferior possession to be used in whatever way he needs. In fact, in married-bachelor circles, Galatians 3:28 is interpreted this way: In Christ there is neither male nor female. But among men, women are inferior.

The married bachelor is also rigid and uncompromising. He believes that his position as head gives him the God-given right to direct and control his wife. He is the conqueror, she the conquered. He barks, she jumps. In his mind he has purchased her, for he has provided a roof over her head, children, and financial support. In return she should obey him unquestioningly and satisfy his every demand. If she disobeys him he has the God-given right to punish her and force compliance as you would with a dog. This couple can spend a lifetime coexisting as long as the wife never disagrees. The constant question in their home is, "Who is in charge?" For her emotional and physical safety the answer had better be, "You are, dear."

Ann Landers once printed a letter from Big Ed, who stated that some women are like dumb animals. You have to show them who's boss. He said he was training his right from the beginning, "and believe me, there are no arguments in our house. This is the way all families ought to be run." And all the married bachelors said, "Amen."

What would you do if your family needed to move into another home? You'd begin looking for another home together, wouldn't you? Not the married bachelor! He would go out on his own and find a house that fit his specifications. Only then would he inform his family where they would soon be privileged to live.

One such man loved his horses, so he went out to find the perfect place where he could board the horses and house his family. He found the property, put the deposit down, and then took his wife to see it. The only trouble was it had one less bedroom than they had children, and it was dirty, dark, and dingy. She dared to tell him of her dissatisfaction. His response was to begin yelling. She wrote the tirade down and brought it into the counseling office the next day: "You are just like the serpent," he snapped. "Stop raising your ugly head! Why don't you just be submissive as God intended? You're not just a verbal threat, either. You're an emotional threat to me."

Our spirits grieved with hers that any man, especially one who calls himself a Christian, would choose to treat another human being with such disrespect. If one person in a relationship needs to have his/her way constantly, it resembles a puppeteer working a puppet.

This spiritualized female put-down is thoroughly unbiblical! In his thought-provoking book *The Mystery of Marriage*, Mike Mason writes these words:

> "A man's home is his castle," goes the saying, and in practice this is taken to mean that a man is allowed and even encouraged to develop into any sort of despot or devil he likes within the cozy confines, the cordoned lawlessness, of his own family. After all, aren't his loved ones those who "understand" and "accept" him? And so marriage becomes a form of institutionalized complacency, a hothouse of mutually nourished neuroses. Love is even construed to be a sort of carte blanche approval for all kinds of selfishness and evil, a dispensation giving two people special license to sin against one another.[3]

The Dependent Female: I'm the Little Woman!

In this horribly demeaning relationship, the married bachelor puts all his efforts into getting his partner, his "little woman," to behave. (In some cases the married bachelor is a wife who dominates her husband. Most often the dominant partner is male, however.) There is just one perspective voiced in this type of marriage, and it reflects not a loving interaction but a monologue.

This is where the dependent, submissive, doormat little woman finds herself. She is used by her partner to be a need filler. If he has a need, she had better fill it. She is smothered in this relationship to the extent that she feels like another one of her husband's possessions. If she has value to him, it is to meet his needs and to affirm his perspective as the correct one. And even though she may resent this situation, she feels valuable only when she pleases him.

One such woman shared with us that when she gave up her name to become Mrs. Smith, she also gave up her identity. From that day on she tried to avoid rejection by attempting to constantly please her mate. We knew her husband, and so we knew she had committed herself to an impossible task.

She would tell of returning home from church or a social gathering with him, and suddenly she'd realize she must have done something to upset him. He would never tell her what it was but she could tell he was angry by the way he was driving. Her punishment was consistent: there was no attention and no affection until she'd paid penance for her mistake. It could take her literally days to figure out what she had done. Perhaps she had laughed too loud or had disagreed with his parents. In the beginning she would plead with him to tell her so she wouldn't repeat her mistake. But he'd stare past her as if she didn't exist and piously ask, "Don't you know?"

Other husbands verbally reinforce their belief that they have married inferior women. This type of husband psychologically abuses his wife by calling her every derogatory name in the book. If she's intelligent, he'll tell her she's stupid. If she's beautiful, she'll be told she's ugly. If she's highly talented, he'll see to it she doesn't exercise her talents outside the home. He verbally assassinates her to maintain control. It is usually just a matter of time before she begins to doubt herself and believe her husband's words. But even worse, she eventually believes that she really is inferior and her only value will come as she proves her value to him. This is the woman who in her heart of hearts is lonely for a part of herself. The part she feels forced to submerge in the presence of her husband is the part that might cause him great displeasure. Big tears fall down her cheeks sometimes, and she can't explain why.

She feels devalued because she must always be the one to give in. Her preferences are compromised and her opinions are either no longer sought or considered less important than others.' She often finds herself cast in the role of scapegoat and she has gotten all too used to being yelled at. It's the public ridicule at church and in front of her friends that is the hardest to take.

At home she feels judged, misunderstood, and underestimated. But worst of all, she feels used and unloved.

One woman wrote us of her situation. Her husband is a prominent elder in the church, well respected, and sought out by many as a spiritual leader. Behind the closed doors of their home it is another story. He not only physically abuses her, he has persuaded her by the misuse of Scripture that she is responsible for all of his problems. He even claims that he hears the voice of God. She feels so emotionally beaten down that she is incapable of challenging his wild claims. This woman and many like her are existing in a living hell.

Think of it! This woman has built her life around her husband. She has attempted to fit his image of the perfect Christian wife. He is an insatiable monster whose needs will never be completely met. Yet she is so terrified of rejection that she can't say no to anything her husband wants. She is at his beck and call twenty-four hours a day.

But all is not miserable. The dependent female often feels cared for and safe. She has not been forced to grow up because she moved right out of her parents' home and into her husband's home. She feels spiritual when she uses self-blame and self-punishment, for she equates guilt and condemnation with spirituality. She also doesn't have to work at setting goals to change her attitudes, thoughts, feelings, or actions. All she has to do is be her husband's robot.

There is a small step separating being controlled and being controlling, and it's dangerous. How many times have you heard a woman say, "He may be the head of this home, but I'm the neck that moves the head." Often these women are the pussycat manipulators who resent their own lack of control to the extent that they get back at their men—any way they can.

And these women have power! Their most lethal weapons of control are manipulation and retaliation, while pretending submission. They seek personal security in their men but indulge, flatter, and attempt to buy them any way they can.

One manipulative method involves babying their men. These little women refuse to be honest about any issue or conflict and protect their men from self-understanding. Why do they baby them? They are terrified of change.

They can be dishonest with their words and actions. One woman we know claims to be submissive and a follower while she destroys her husband's financial base by wasting their money with unwise purchases. She actually charged ten thousand dollars on their credit cards following a major put-down by her husband.

Other women choose to talk disparagingly to their husbands by constantly reminding them that they haven't shaped up to fit their expectations. Some women subtly shame their men, use sex to manipulate them, tears to hurt them, silence to frustrate them, and guilt trips to condemn them. Others choose depression to ostracize them, self-pity, nagging, and bursts of anger to overwhelm them, and a poor state of health to blackmail them.

These women have become masters of manipulation, almost in self-defense, for no man or woman can experience emotional health when their very personhood is defined by someone else.

The Two-Headed Monster: I'm Most Important

In response to the male misuse of headship, many women have chosen to become aggressive and competitive, which imitates the worst in men. They are not remotely interested in submission. Instead they are terribly concerned about a trade-off in domination.

An extraordinarily successful businesswoman we know keeps her finances totally separate from those of her husband. If she wants something for herself or their home, and he is opposed in any way to the purchase, she uses her own funds to acquire it. They are running on opposite tracks. Externally they look as if they've got it all together but the philosophy underlying their marital structure is, "Whoever does the payin' gets the sayin'."

This is not a problem new to our generation. Why, it's as old as Eve herself. When Eve was created God placed her in a beautiful environment with Adam. God intended for them to be partners, created in His image. Together they were to rule over "the fish of the sea, the birds of the air and over every living creature that moves on the ground" (*see* Genesis 1:26).

You are aware of what happened: Eve was deceived. She questioned God's word, set aside her partnership role, and proceeded to dominate her man, and lead him astray. And women have been striving to be one up ever since.

In God's plan, women are not to become like men—regardless of what Henry Higgins sings in *My Fair Lady*. Men, on the other hand, are not to become like women. All of us need to become more Christlike. What a radical difference that would make in our marriages!

THE UNHEALTHY HIERARCHY

Married Bachelor	marries	Submissive Wife
"I'm the head."		"I'm the little woman."
#1 = me.		#1 = him.
Independent.		Dependent.
"Life is built around me."		"Life is built around my mate."
"What I want is most important."		"What he wants is most important."

THE ISOLATE RELATIONSHIP
OR
TWO-HEADED MONSTER

Married Bachelor	marries	Married Bachelor
"I'm the head."		"I'm the head."
#1 = me.		#1 = me.
Independent.		Independent.
"Life is built around me."		"Life is built around me."
"What I want is most important."		"What I want is most important."

3

Making Your Marriage Come Alive

FROM THE LOVE OF POWER TO THE POWER OF LOVE

*The most frequent earthquakes are
inner ones. They are needed to break
up a belief "foundation" so that
a better one may be built.*

DOROTHY CORKILLE BRIGGS [1]

After observing other Christian marriages and facing our own frustrations head-on, we chose to get back to the Scriptures. As a result we had to face the truth that Jesus had become an addition to our relationship rather than central in it.

There is not a human being alive who controls himself, even though the media are constantly bombarding us with the lie that we do. Whatever is lord of our lives controls us. The woman who lives her life script in hopes of being accepted by her husband is controlled by that very husband. The man or woman who lives to "do it my way" ends up controlled by ego, by power, and by inflexibility.

In our study we came across some words that both of us

had forgotten: "Worship the Lord your God and serve Him only" (*see* Deuteronomy 6:13). Why is the Lord to be Lord of our lives? The answer becomes clear when we consider the options. The Lord is the only one who controls us without destroying us. In fact, when Jesus is Lord of our lives, we find ourselves.

In dependent and independent relationships one partner has replaced Christ as the other partner's authority. Therefore, if you cling to dependency, you seek caretakers. You make those imperfect human beings your god and you resent them. If you cling to independence, you make yourself your god and you seek people to be "need fillers" for you. After a while you realize their imperfections and you abandon them. This is the result of man's sinfulness, not the result of God's commands.

James H. Olthuis writes:

> Sin distorted the relation between man and woman. . . . No longer a helpmate, woman would become a competitor rather than a companion. Man would take advantage of the woman's natural yearning for him in order to rule over her. . . .
>
> Thus, what has been called the battle of the sexes is actually the abnormal result of the Fall. Man-in-sin will attempt to dominate woman as if she were just a part of the creation to be put under his feet; yet man himself is also cursed and the entire creation with him. . . .
>
> It is important to emphasize that the curses of the Lord are just that—curses, not commands to be obeyed. They are the Lord's infallible description of mankind's future in sin . . . the words of the curse are not norms to guide our male-female relations.[2]

We are to live by the words of the new commandment, not the curse: ". . . Love one another. As I have loved you, so you must love one another" (John 13:34). That is an impossible command from a human standpoint. There is only one possibility to love unqualifiedly and to forgive unconditionally, and that is if Jesus Christ, the ultimate expression of love, is the supreme authority in our lives.

If we are using the words of the curse as a self-fulfilling prophecy and as a justification for extreme selfishness, then we *love power*. In God's plan we will discover the *power of love*. There is an overwhelming difference:

LOVE OF POWER	POWER OF LOVE
Focus on me	Focus on us
Emphasis on getting	Emphasis on giving
Dominates	Serves
Demands	Discusses
Negates others	Encourages others
Reacts	Responds
Corrupts	Empowers
Uses	Frees
Self-motivated	Christ-enabled

In order to understand the power of love, we discovered we had to change our thinking in four areas.

Shed Selfishness

There is a tremendous cost involved if we are willing to love as Jesus Christ loved. We have to give up our extraordinary selfishness. We may find it necessary to admit our desire to be leader rather than lover. When we marry, we choose to give our love to another human being. What we give up, if ours is a Christian marriage, is our right to be a totally independent entity.

Shed Prejudices

Not only must we ask the Holy Spirit to help us shed our selfishness, we must also examine our prejudices. There are no "little" women, no "little" people in Christ's kingdom. God, through Christ's death on the cross, established the equal value of both male and female. In Galatians 3:28 we read, "There is neither Jew nor Greek, slave nor free, male nor female, for you are all one in Christ Jesus."

Christ's death on the cross settled once and for all the issue of our identity. Each of us was declared highly significant, deeply fallen, and greatly loved. The cross literally leveled both husbands and wives before their Savior, and each must make an individual response to Christ's offer of salvation.

Shed False Ideas of Headship

We must, if scriptural, accept the full personhood of both male and female. The Bible does not put down either men or women, just sin in both.

What it does say is that "the husband is the head of the wife as Christ is the head of the church, his body, of which he is the Savior" (Ephesians 5:23). But we must shed the idea that headship is synonymous with power. We believe it means the husband is head, yes—but within a relationship of equals. His headship is not exercised so he can glory in feelings of superiority. It is exercised for his partner's benefit.

We seem to be fascinated with the pecking order of things. Christ never was. In Mark 10:35–45 there is an interesting interchange between Jesus and the sons of Zebedee. James and John boldly ask Jesus if they can sit on either side of Him in glory. Jesus informs them that they don't know what they are asking.

It doesn't take long for word of this conversation to filter back to the other disciples. They are ticked! They probably let James and John have it in no uncertain terms. Jesus gets wind of the conflict and these are His words in verses 42–45:

> . . . "You know that those who are regarded as rulers of the Gentiles lord it over them, and their high officials exercise authority over them. Not so with you. Instead, whoever wants to become great among you must be your servant, and whoever wants to be first must be slave of all. For even the Son of Man did not come to be served, but to serve, and to give his life as a ransom for many."

Headship does not mean one-upmanship. In reality it is one-downmanship.

Christ, the Head, is our prime example of a servant. In Philippians 2:5–8 we discover that Christ was equal with God yet He emptied Himself of power and took on the form of a slave. Picture for a moment God washing the dirty feet of His disciples or allowing Himself to be hung on a tree.

Christian husbands must follow His example and become servants, not bosses. They must have deep, unselfish, self-sacrificing love for their wives, just as Christ has for the Church.

There is no way husbands can ignore the command to submit to their wives. Ephesians 5:21 comes before all the verses on headship. In Christ's life, submission and love were synonymous. To love is to serve! Apparently that was as radical a thought in the time of Christ as it seems to be today.

Are you controlled by
the love of power
or
are you living out
the power of love?

Love—not power—is Christ's way. We are called to outdo one another in love, not power. That's a whole lot different from the man who comes in for counseling, slams his thick Bible down on our desk with a crash, and lashes out, "If she'd only submit, our marriage would be fine!" If husbands feel they must demand submission and if they find themselves angry a great deal of the time, then they're more concerned with having their needs met than with being servants.

How do we imitate Christ? First of all, we acknowledge that we are equal before God. We lay aside our concept of headship as synonymous with power. We relinquish our "right" to control and manipulate another human being and we take on the form of a servant in our relationships. Willingly, we affirm our spouses in their journeys toward wholeness and completeness rather than viewing their journeys as a threat.

Six times in the Gospels we read that the greatest must be a servant (*see* Matthew 20:26–28, 23:11; Mark 9:35, 10:43–45; Luke 9:48, 22:26, 27). Paul spends nine verses exhorting husbands to love their wives, while he directs only four verses to the wives. Perhaps the husbands were having a difficult time accepting this command.

The need for servanthood is crystal clear. It is impossible to share our faith in Jesus Christ by word or by example with someone we are treating as a doormat, with someone we have placed on a pedestal, or with someone we are exploiting, manipulating, or using to meet our needs.

Something in all of us fights being a servant, and it's often at this point that we find ourselves procrastinating in the initiation of love. Herein is discipleship fought out: our will versus God's. Are we committed to God's way or aren't we? We hope your answer is, "I will be a servant in my marriage regardless of my spouse's response or lack of it." That's the commitment that mutual submission makes.

Shed False Ideas of Submission

Both husband and wife in a Christ-centered marriage are called to mutual love and mutual submission. They are each exhorted to serve the other. Ephesians 5:22, the passage in which wives are commanded to submit to their husbands, must be understood in the context of Ephesians 5:21, which stresses *mutual* submission. We are to yield to each other, interact with each other, and listen to each other. In addition, we are to yield together, interact together, and listen together to the Lord.

Ephesians 5:22 (wives submit) is followed by Ephesians 5:25 (husbands love). Colossians 3:18 (wives submit) is followed by Colossians 3:19: ("Husbands, love your wives and do not be harsh with them"). The mutuality of the marriage relationship becomes obvious. Both husbands and wives are exhorted to serve each other in love.

We believe that each married couple sets a pattern for the entire Christian community. If we can't serve our partners, whom can we serve? If we can't love our partners, whom can we love? If we can't submit to our partners, to whom can we submit?

There is so much confusion tied to the word *submission.* Scriptural submission is a positive, voluntary result of putting Christ first and being filled by the Holy Spirit. Elaine Stedman defines it this way:

Authentic submission is not reluctant nor grudging, nor is it the result of imposed authority. It is rather a chosen, deliberate, voluntary, love-initiated response to another's need. It is an act of worship to God, whom we serve in serving others. In no way, then, is authentic submission a violation of our humanity. It is appropriate to the purpose for which we were created, since in serving His creatures we are serving and worshiping our Creator. And it acknowledges the dignity of our humanity because it is service freely rendered from a will surrendered to the loving purposes of God.[3]

Submission is voluntary—a personal choice—and it is only possible for those men and women who have a strong understanding of who they are in Jesus Christ. It is only possible between two people who are aware of their equality before God and each other.

Mutual submission results from an awareness that in serving others, we are really serving and worshiping our God. Therefore, both members in the relationship will do their best to free each other to be all that God wants them to be. Each partner tries to surrender as much as possible for the sake of the other. Each one commits himself/herself to be God's instrument of unconditional love to his/her partner.

Nowhere in Scripture does subjection mean inferiority. Christ was subject unto His parents (*see* Luke 2:51). In 1 Corinthians 15:28, Christ subjects Himself to His Father. Then Peter, in 1 Peter 5:5, exhorts people to subject themselves to their elders and to one another, even as he warns the elders not to lord it over their flocks. Submitting to one another does not involve the idea of inferiority. Rather, it is a call to serve each other in order to fulfill God's requirements for a growing relationship.

What is your perspective about submission? If you are a married bachelor, your view will be quite different from that held by a dependent partner who equates the term *submission* with a picture of a doormat. On this chart we have laid out the contrasting viewpoints about submission that we discussed in the preceding chapters. Can you place yourself and your partner on this chart?

EXAMINING SUBMISSION

Dependent	*Independent*	*Interdependent*
1. Submits out of duty, guilt, or laziness. Reluctant, grudging, sometimes pretending.	1. Refuses to submit and rebels against it.	1. Submits out of choice. Chosen, deliberate, voluntary, love initiated, mutually submissive.
2. Results from imposed authority.	2. Refuses to submit or uses it for manipulation.	2. Responds to another's need. Act of worship to God, whom we serve in serving our mates.
3. Doormat mentality. Partner is on a pedestal. Negates self.	3. Power mentality. Submission is a trade-off in domination.	3. Christlike mentality. Power is laid aside to serve.
4. Gives up everything. Gives in to the spouse.	4. Gives in order to get.	4. Gives out of love.

God's way is a partnership of equals, each recognizing Jesus Christ as Source, each submitting in love to the other, and each serving the other with joy. We call this an *interdependent* or *partnership* marriage.

These statements are designed to help you evaluate your attitudes and actions. As you prayerfully consider them, take the time to affirm your positive progress with a check mark. Place an X by the statements in which you want to experience growth:

_____ I treat my partner as if he/she is my equal.

_____ I have a servant's heart.

_____ I listen to my spouse's opinions and complaints without threat.

_____ I'm willing to give up something I want to do in order to do something my partner wants to do.

_____ I make reasonable requests of my partner.

_____ I'm available to help my spouse around our home.

_____ I try to make life pleasant for my spouse.

_____ I genuinely care about my partner's feelings, thoughts, dreams, and questions.

_____ I set my spouse free to develop his/her gifts and talents.

_____ I own my emotions, expressions, experiences, actions, happiness or lack of it.

_____ I treat my partner with respect.

_____ I am on guard so that "little" things do not develop into the unhealthy kinds of patterns that undermine a relationship.

_____ I help with the children.

_____ I am aware of my spouse's talents and temperament and I leave him/her free to use these strengths inside and outside our home.

_____ I put Christ first in my life.

We must be willing to shed our selfishness, our prejudices, and our false ideas of headship and submission. By following Jesus Christ's example of sacrificial, serving love, we exchange our human love of power and begin, in this most intimate relationship, to live out the power of love.

This chart contrasts the results you will evidence in your marriage, depending on whether you choose to be a dependent, independent, or interdependent person.

MUTUAL SUBMISSION WALKED OUT

Dependent	*Independent*	*Interdependent*
Value my spouse.	Value myself.	Value myself and my spouse equally as God's persons.
Dependency on spouse.	Dependency on self.	Dependency on Jesus Christ.
Increased feelings of inferiority.	Increased feelings of superiority.	Increased feelings of self-respect.
In bondage to my spouse's expectations.	I create expectations everyone else must fill.	Freed us up to be ourselves.
Wear masks and pretend agreement.	Wear masks.	Become real and honest.
Listener.	Better talker than listener.	Good listener and communicator.

MUTUAL SUBMISSION WALKED OUT

Dependent	*Independent*	*Interdependent*
Prayer—confession only.	Prayer—who needs it?	Prayer—shared vulnerability before God.
Interested in your growth.	I grow.	Mutual growth.
I am a responder in our sexual relationship.	I initiate.	Both initiate physical intimacy.
My spouse's responsibility to determine our marital style—live by someone else's formula.	I determine my own style.	Assume personal responsibility for the style of our marriage—live by our joint formula.
Children—my total responsibility.	Children—someone else's responsibility.	Children—our responsibility.
Home—my responsibility.	Home—your responsibility.	Home—our responsibility.
Manipulation is alive and well.	Manipulation is alive and well.	Manipulation comes to a swift halt.

MUTUAL SUBMISSION WALKED OUT

Dependent	*Independent*	*Interdependent*
My spouse has the opportunities.	I have the opportunities.	We are equal in opportunities.
I submit out of duty.	You submit because I have other things to do.	We both submit out of love.

That's our assignment for the remainder of our married lives. We are to be Christ's channels of love to our partners. In the process of doing this, we will learn that loving the Father is done by loving the dear people we married. This is something that only we can do as Christ's channel of love to our mates. This is a wondrous commitment on which we embark.

In the second section of our book we will consider the practical ways to begin living as interdependent people in our marriages. The benefits of mutual submission will both challenge and encourage you to begin experiencing the life-style of love.

The result will be a deep understanding of God's love for us, a growth in the depth of our love for God, and an increasing sense of being God's person for our mates in this place and time. We are God's love connection to the person we chose to marry.

THE PARTNERSHIP
OR
INTERDEPENDENT MARRIAGE

A	marries	A
Self-respecting person.		Self-respecting person.
"Christ is my head."		"Christ is my head."
#1 = Christ.		#1 = Christ.
Interdependent (life built around Christ).		Interdependent (life built around Christ).
"I want what is best for our relationship under God."		"I want what is best for our relationship under God."

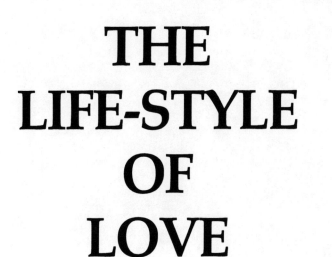

THE
LIFE-STYLE
OF
LOVE

4

How to Get Over the Need to Change Your Mate

FROM ATTACKER TO ACCEPTER

I'm thankful for David. For reasons I can't always understand he loves me. He has seen the secret parts of me, the blunders I have made, the insecurities I still carry, and he accepts me. It is an amazing thing to have been loved for sixteen years by someone I so respect. The astonishing reality is that he loves me, even when his eyes are open wide.

A friend had a dream one evening. In it her husband was lying on an operating table in a local hospital. The surgeon was none other than Jesus Christ. He turned and addressed our friend: "You also are in this operating room. I am using you to bring healing in the life of your husband."

"Lord, what am I?" asked our friend. "Surely I'm not the scalpel You're using to cut out the cancerous sores in my husband?"

"No, that is not your use," replied her Savior. "Look again."

Our friend's eyes scanned the operating theater. Could she be the heart machine, the operating table, the light? Each time the reply came back negative. Suddenly she saw something she hadn't seen before.

"Lord, am I the IV?"

"Yes, My child. I'm counting on you to keep the clear, life-building nourishment coming to this man you married."

With that our friend awakened. She was struck by the fact that often she had chosen to be the scalpel in her husband's life, taking it upon herself to cut out his irritating habits and strange idiosyncrasies. What could that mean? How had she gotten into the habit of being the scalpel?

Accept the Need for Change

Perhaps it had happened way back when she and her favorite guy were dating. Adulthood holds its own fantasies. She had spent hours dreaming about this guy she was going to marry. They had so much in common. He was going to save her from an unfulfilling life. He might only have driven a Volkswagen but he was her prince, howbeit a modern one.

Rose DeWolf puts it this way:

We've come up with some tough standards of our own for men. He must be brave in the face of danger ("The bullet only went through my shoulder, ma'am; nothin' to fret about") but also warm and vulnerable. He must be protective, yet not overbearing. He must always be there when we need him, yet understand that we need time for ourselves. He should be good-looking, adventurous, and sexy, but also faithful and a good father. He should be successful and respected in the community, but spend most of his time with us. He should be cool and strong, yet hot and lively. He should be brilliant and creative but never bored when we are less so, or annoyed when we are more so. He should feel we are totally his equal and yet, if there is a noise downstairs at night, he should find out what it is. He should make a very nice living, but value our contribution. He must not only place his cloak in the mud . . . but thereafter take it to the cleaners himself.[1]

The fantasies and expectations our friend built in her mind were completely unrealistic and totally unobtainable. She fell in love with the fantasy and not the man.

Our friend is not unusual. Men and women enter marriage laden with excess baggage. Some expectations are created as a result of the home we were raised in, some as a result of the television programs and movies we watched, and some as a result of the church we attended or chose not to attend. The vast majority of us marry a fantasy.

It seems to take approximately six months for our partners to get bad breath, but one morning we wake up and, boy, do they ever have halitosis! The quirks that seemed so endearing during courtship suddenly become signs of severe adult neuroses.

One of the tasks of early marriage is to figure out who the person you married really is (even if he/she has been your next-door neighbor since preschool). There is so much you don't know. It's inevitable he'll crave prime rib just when you can think of nothing but Chinese food. She will be in the mood for a romantic rendezvous when you are in the mood for sleep. One of you will want to vacation in Alaska and one of you in Australia.

As God's love connection,
can we refuse to open
our arms,
our thinking,
our loving?

Accept Reality

At that moment we are all faced with a choice. Can we accept reality as it is, and go with it, or are we going to become a scalpel in our mate's life, trying to remove all aggravating characteristics? It is the tendency of 99 percent of us to make our mates into a renovation project. The other 1 percent just won't admit the desire. Stop and write down the fantasies you both nurtured before your marriage:

_____

_____

_____

_____

_____

_____

_____

_____

We know that neither partner should presume that he/she knows what is best for the other and insist that he/she be that way. But we do it anyway. If we think we know something, but we don't do it, then we don't yet know it.

Have you ever thought, *My partner is not who I thought he/she was*? Have you felt disillusionment? Perhaps you need to ask yourself who created the illusion. Your partner is who your partner is. We all need to be given the chance to be ourselves.

Why are we threatened by differences in our mates? If we're honest, we're afraid that our little bubbles of security will burst. We might have to adjust our ways of thinking, of doing things, of seeing our world. That rocks the boat.

There is also another reason. Secretly we believe that if it's different, it's suspect and even wrong. But that very fear is destructive to a relationship. Leo Buscaglia writes:

> To bring another into our life in love we must be willing to give up certain destructive characteristics. For example:
> The need to be always right.
> The need to be first in everything.
> The need to be constantly in control.
> The need to be perfect.
> The need to be loved by everyone.
> The need to possess.
> The need to be free of conflict and
>   frustration.
> The need to change others for our
>   needs.
> The need to manipulate.
> The need to blame.
> The need to dominate.[2]

This list sounds as if it has something to do with abandoning the love of power and discovering the power of love. It sounds a great deal like 1 Corinthians 13, the love chapter of the Bible. Can it be that our relationship with God determines our relationship with our mates?

Accept Marriage as a Ministry

In whose eyes is your mate unacceptable? Is it possible that you are looking through the wrong eyes? When God looks at people, He sees them as highly significant and loves them greatly, even though they are deeply fallen.

God loves us in spite of who we are. Romans 5:8 puts it this way: "But God demonstrates his own love for us in this: While we were still sinners, Christ died for us." We are loved by God and special to God even with all of our quirks.

Is it possible that when we focus only on our mates' differences and weaknesses, this may be a mirror for our own feelings of insecurity? As we grow in the knowledge that we are totally accepted by God and deeply loved, we can begin to like ourselves. This will free us to accept others.

One of our main goals in marriage needs to be to minister to our mates in a way that will emphasize what God has done for us in Jesus Christ. God, through acceptance, has given us a feeling of value, a knowledge of love, and has declared our self-worth. We, as the love connection, the IV from God Himself, do the same thing for our mates. We do something nice for them. We don't try to change them.

To share life with another person and to accept each other with ever-deepening understanding is the highest goal of marriage. It certainly beats the distancing, destroying, degrading, and devaluing that happens when we refuse to accept our marriage partners.

Marriage is not only a ministry to our mates, it is also a ministry to God. The way we accept and encourage our mates, the way we respond to our mates, the way we free our mates, are all ways we minister to the Lord. When we don't accept our mates as a gift from God's hand, we're accusing God of gross mismanagement of our lives.

Love is always open arms.[3] If we close our arms about love we are left holding only ourselves. What is the ultimate symbol of open arms? It is Jesus Christ on the cross of Calvary. As His love connection to the person we married, can we refuse to open our arms, our thinking, and our loving?

Eve was made for Adam because it was not good for him to be alone. Yet there are many mates who would rather be alone than with their nonaccepting spouses. Does your mate think that he/she is fortunate because you are his/her partner?

There is no greater way of expressing love for your partner than by allowing individuality. In a loving relationship you have to live with each other as you are. It doesn't mean that you are never going to change. But it does mean it probably won't happen in the foreseeable future. Contrary to popular opinion, marriage is not a reform school.

Certainly there is the possibility of being "a new creation in Christ" (*see* 2 Corinthians 5:17) and of ". . . forgetting what is behind and straining toward what is ahead, I press on toward the goal to win the prize for which God has called me heavenward in Christ Jesus" (Philippians 3:13, 14). But nagging, pouting and condemnation won't get your mate there. The absolute worst way to improve our mates is to condemn them. Judgment breeds bondage, which brings restraint, causes confusion, paralysis, and pain, makes division, and locks up potential. Natalie Wood was once quoted as saying, "The only time a woman truly succeeds in changing a man is when he's a baby."

The marriage relationship is a partnership with God and under God. It is not a slip of ownership. The husband is not to own his wife; he is to love her as Christ loves the Church. The wife is not to own her husband; she is to respect him. We can't change people. What we can change is our attitude toward people.

All Dave's good qualities drew Jan to him—his quiet, thoughtful, gentle, deep ways. After about six months, she wondered why he wasn't more like her. Couldn't he do anything impulsively? Couldn't he get excited and didn't he have anything to say?

A similar experience happened to Dave. He fell in love with those flashy eyes and the spirited, strong-willed woman, only to be shocked a few months later when the eyes flashed in anger rather than delight. It didn't take him long to label the strong will: stubbornness.

One day Jan was reading Matthew 20:20–28. This is the story of the mother of Zebedee's sons coming to Jesus to request that Jimmy sit on one side of Him in heaven and Johnny sit on the other side. As Jan read this she thought, *Imagine that, telling Jesus what to do. What nerve!* At that moment a quiet impression settled in her mind. "That, Jan, is what you are doing to Dave. You are telling Me what kind of a man he needs to become. Believe Me, I will do a much better job of maturing him than you will."

Jan went to Dave and repented of her mother-superior attitude. Dave confessed his tendency to want Jan to be a revised standard version of himself. We still stumble but the good news is that the confessions come much quicker now.

Marriage consists of learning to live and love without rose-colored glasses. Real people are more fun than fantasies. They are infinitely more interesting than our creations would have been. A woman wrote to *Reader's Digest* in 1977 and her comments bear repeating: "Early in our marriage, we learned to see through each other . . . and still enjoy the view!"

Marriages are happy when partners are able to abandon their original expectations. Expectations can be a trap. But what are we supposed to do with them? We like Anne Ortlund's answer.

> *Don't abandon your expectations.* (The solution isn't to expect little or nothing; you'd get bored in a hurry.) Don't abandon your expectations—*shift them. . . . God Himself, in Jesus Christ, is the only secure, safe foundation for a great marriage.*
>
> You want stars in your eyes. You want great dreams together. All right, *ask Him* for all the good things you want from your marriage.[4]

Expect more from God. Accept your mate with open arms.

We are back to God again. Our relationship to God has everything to do with our relationship with that man or woman we married. The chart on page 68 demonstrates that if our identities are based on God's love for us, then we are free to accept others. If our identities are found either in our spouses or through ourselves, we can only manipulate our spouses to fit our expectations.

As God's love connection to our mates, we are to demonstrate in a concrete way that our mates have value to us, just the way they are, regardless of their performances. At this point love becomes a choice, not a feeling.

God loved, and as a result, He gave. The Son of God came to minister and give His life as a ransom for many. In imitation of Christ and because of the power of the Holy Spirit, we are to choose to concentrate more on what we can bring to our marriage relationships rather than what we can get from them.

Accept a New Perspective

As a way of living out God's unconditional love to our partners, we can chose to bring a new perspective to our relationships. In the space provided below, answer this question: How do you differ from your spouse?

_____

_____

_____

_____

_____

_____

_____

_____

We look at the world from our own points of view. We are familiar with our perspective and so comfortable with it that we might even call it the right perspective. Do we dare point out that there is another way of looking at things? There are both discouraging and encouraging ways to view differences.

Do you communicate acceptance of and respect for your mate's differences? Is your perspective of him/her negative and judgmental? Is it possible that your "argumentative" spouse loves a good discussion? Could your "quiet" spouse be a thinker and an excellent listener?

At this point we suggest you take the list you just created and discover the positive perspective about those differences.

Differences Considered Negative	*Positive Alternative*

DIFFERING VIEWS
OF ACCEPTANCE

	Dependent	*Independent*	*Interdependent*
IDENTITY FOUND	Through my spouse.	Through myself.	Through grasping God's love and acceptance.
VIEW OF SELF	Lacking self-esteem: "I am nothing."	Inflated: "I am all that I need."	Positive and realistic: "I am highly significant, deeply fallen, greatly loved."
VIEW OF OTHERS	Worships them, threatened by them, clings to them.	Uses them to meet my needs.	Values them.
CAN I ACCEPT DIFFERENCES?	Pushes for uniformity, security, critical of self and partner.	Pushes for uniformity, will expose, critical of partner.	Accepts as I have been accepted, complements.

Do you dare to go one step further? What would happen if you asked, "Lord, did You have something in mind for my growth when You brought my partner with this quality to our marriage? Why does it aggravate me so? Is it pointing out an area in which I need to grow?

Perhaps your wife is overtalkative. Has that delivered you from being a noncommunicative bore? Perhaps your partner is extremely quiet. Have you increased in your ability to draw him/her out? Have you become an excellent listener?

How long has it been since you affirmed to God that you receive or accept your mate as a gift from Him, a gift meant to stretch you? Do you dare to make a written affirmation of this truth in the space provided below?

_____

_____

_____

_____

_____

_____

_____

_____

Once we stop condemning and start accepting, we come to the realization that as a couple we're better together than either of us is separately. In our relationship, Dave's strengths help Jan's weaknesses and vice versa. Mutual respect is the basis for any healthy relationship.

What does acceptance do? It releases our partners from the fear of being condemned. It models the love of Christ, it breeds acceptance, releases our partners to grow, settles confusion, breaks down barriers, and broadens our perspective.

True love says, "I love you unconditionally, not only for

the privilege of loving you but for what loving you makes of me." We have a choice: we can complain and prolong our misery, or we can receive our mates as God's gifts to us. If you choose to accept your mate in this way, we invite you to make these affirmations with us.

I accept _____ as he/she is.
         (mate's name)

I relinquish any hidden agendas for him/her.

I liberate _____ to be all he/she can
         (mate's name)
possibly be, all that You make him/her to be.

I will stop being my mate's Holy Spirit.

I accept _____ differences as part of Your
         (your mate's name)
refining process in my life.

From this time forth, I will choose to view his/her differences in a positive manner.

I accept _____ as Your gift to me
         (mate's name)
so together we can be all that You want us to be.

5

How to Bring Out the Best in Both of You

FROM ADVERSARY TO AFFIRMER

*Relationships seldom die because they suddenly
have no life in them. They wither slowly,
either because people do not understand how
much or what kind of upkeep, time, work,
love and caring they require or because people
are too lazy or afraid to try. A relationship
is a living thing. It needs and benefits
from the same attention to detail that an
artist lavishes on his art.*

DR. DAVID VISCOTT[1]

When we love someone, as Christ loves, we accept him/her with no preconditions. The commitment to love unconditionally sets both free to grow, to learn, and yes, even to change. We do not love our mates in order to change them. If we do, our love has become conditional, and we have become power hungry.

We love our spouses because they are:

- created in God's image
- individuals in process
- significant to God
- greatly loved by God
- unique

Humorist Harry Golden used to tell the tale of Mrs. Lipshitz, who wore a diamond the size of an egg. A friend commented that Mrs. L. was certainly lucky to have such a fabulous jewel. "True," said Mrs. Lipshitz, "but of course, you realize that along with the Lipshitz Diamond comes the Lipshitz Curse."

"And what is it?" her friend asked of Mrs. Lipshitz.

"Mr. Lipshitz," came the reply.[2]

Do you see your mate as a royal pain in the neck or do you see him/her as a precious, growing, gifted human being?

If you are volunteering to be God's love connection to your mate, you will be willing to follow Christ's example and be an affirmer in your partner's life. You will affirm through both your attitudes and your words.

Affirmation Through Attitudes

The absolute worst way to improve a marriage is to condemn a mate. It will, in fact, take you nowhere. Your spouse will be hurt, angry, and terribly disillusioned, and you will be an arrogant, miserable, and unfulfilled mate.

Spouses who love power misuse affirmation. In their hands affirmation becomes a tool of manipulation to get their spouses to do what they want. It becomes a competitive game rather than a genuine response of love given for the good of the affirmed person.

COMMITTED TO AFFIRMATION

Dependent	*Independent*	*Interdependent*
Because I idolize.	Because I want my own way.	Because I love myself and you.
Out of a belief in the other person's value.	Out of a belief in my value. The other person can be of use to me.	Out of a belief that both of us are valuable.
Can be a tool of manipulation for the giver's personal use.	Can be a tool of manipulation for the giver's personal use.	Given for the good of the affirmed person.
Can be a genuine response to action (performance based).	Can be a genuine response to action (performance based).	Can be a genuine response to action and character (performance and person based).
Feels like a threat; widens the gap.	Competitive threat.	No threat because I see the good in myself too.

How much better to have this attitude of affirmation:

> God, through the years
> Of our married life
> You have been holding a crown
> About ten feet above my husband's head.
> He was simply too busy
> Loving and serving to notice.
> But I saw it
> Not only did I see it—
> I watched him grow into it.[3]

Each of us makes daily choices whether we leave "heartprints" or heartaches on our partner's life. We can choose to notice our partner's strengths. We can choose to see our marriage as satisfying. A positive attitude is contagious. Dr. Robert Schuller writes, "Perfect love perceives people—not as problems! But—as possibilities!"[4] Hope and positivity quickly improve our feelings of satisfaction about our marriages, spouses, and ourselves.

If you are willing to demonstrate God's love to that person you married, pause right now. Bow your head and thank God for bringing him/her into your life. In the space provided below, write down ten things you appreciate about your mate.

_____

_____

_____

_____

_____

_____

_____

_____

_____

_____

We recommend that you keep this list in a special place. Work at adding new appreciations to it on a daily basis. Once or twice a day pray through this list, thanking God for those wonderful characteristics that He has built into your partner. On those days when the love feelings aren't flowing, you will be amazed at the difference this gratitude will make in your attitude. There's another bonus. As you focus on what is good in your spouse, your eyes will be opened to see more.

We are to bless our mates. The word *blessing* in Greek means "well word." That leads us to the next step.

Affirmation Through Words

Does your husband or wife know that you are his or her number-one fan? It is not unusual for a couple to talk carelessly to each other. They react to an assumption rather than responding to reality. We often respond out of habit rather than by choice. In so doing, we miss many opportunities to affirm one another.

As adults desiring to grow toward maturity, we choose to act rather than react. But acting is a conscious decision of our wills. Choose words that are encouraging, loving, affirming, thoughtful, and considerate—whether you feel like it or not. Choose them whether your partner responds or not.

"Why?" you ask. Because loving and caring for our spouses is a way of loving and caring for ourselves. Love has so many benefits, not the least of which is that it increases our own self-esteem. It also gives us a sense of being Christ's person to our mates and it attracts the love of others. We grow by supporting one another's growth.

We will fail miserably in the act of affirmation if we haven't trained ourselves to notice our spouses. None of us is invisible. The opposite of love is not hate; it is indifference. There is nothing worse than feeling the indifference, the coolness from someone we love.

As God's love connection to our mates, we need to be constantly watching, listening, waiting, changing, adjusting, and readjusting. We are not today what we will be tomorrow. Each of us changes ever so subtly over the course of a day. If we fail to notice our spouses, we will surely miss the wonder of who these people we love are becoming.

Jan remembers the time Dave shaved off his moustache. It took Jan two days to notice. Following that embarrassing and comical moment, Jan made a covenant with the Lord to really notice Dave. Do you need to make such a pact? Then why don't you write out a contract (in the space provided below), committing yourself to really notice the person you married.

_____

_____

_____

_____

_____

_____

_____

_____

_____

Now that you have committed yourself to notice one another, you are ready to take the next step: choosing your words carefully.

Keep the words coming:

"I love your body."
"You sure make that suit look good."
"I value your sensitivity."
"I love your smile."
"I'm proud of you."

God looks at us
with
eyes of love.
Can we do
less
for our mates?

We're not mind readers but we can hear some of you now. You are probably thinking, *I couldn't talk that way. I'm shy and I'd feel weird.*

We are going to be bold and suggest that you change your vocabulary. You need to be willing to say, "I didn't used to talk this way but now I do." Marriages don't just naturally grow; they naturally stagnate. Do you remember how much effort and thought you put into dating? If we aren't working at growing our marriages and stretching ourselves, our marriages will be in deep trouble. Our love will die.

Let's go to Christ's life to see how He carried out this principle of affirmation.

Words Spoken Ahead of Schedule. Jesus Christ verbally affirms each person ahead of schedule. Instead of calling us sinners, He refers to us as saints and as children of God. That certainly provides people with some growing space, doesn't it?

When Jesus first met Simon, He looked him straight in the eye and called him *Peter.* What is the difference, you ask? *Simon* meant "reed," someone easily tossed to and fro. *Peter* meant "rock," a symbol of stability. The name was not withheld by Jesus until Peter proved himself. It was given in love so Peter could grow into it. Affirmers see people as they are and accept them. Affirmers also see people as they can become.

Some of the greatest success stories have followed a word of encouragement or an act of confidence by a loved one. We have one of our own. Dave was bogged down with the possibility of finishing his doctoral dissertation in time to graduate. He had spent almost five years pursuing this mutual goal of ours. I [Jan] wasn't about to let him believe that he couldn't pull it off.

Together we discussed what would have to happen to make this dissertation a reality. Dave felt he needed two weeks of uninterrupted study time away from school, home, and family. The arrangements were made, and a few moments before he was to leave, I went running up to him with a piece of paper in my hand. On it were printed these words:

> You are invited to a
> Celebration Dinner
> Honoring
> Dr. David G. Congo
> Saturday, May 28, 1983
> Seven in the evening
> at the home of
> Janet and David Congo

After informing him that I had had twenty-five of these invitations printed up, I gave Dave a big hug and sent him off to finish his dissertation. Teasingly I told him that I knew he had a little Scottish blood in him and wouldn't want to waste the money! Laughing, Dave hugged me and thanked me for believing in him. Guess what? He finished.

Words Spoken Directly. Affirmation needs to be given ahead of time but we also learn from watching Christ's life that it needs to be given directly. Jesus didn't go to James and John to tell them about Peter's potential. He spoke directly to Peter.

Author John Powell was crying at his father's deathbed when a nurse tried to console him. He responded by telling the nurse that he was sad his father had died but had been prepared for the death, due to an extended illness. "The reason I'm crying," said John Powell, "is because my father never told me he loved me."

Have you told your mate recently that you love him/her? The best way to compliment your spouse is *frequently*. Don't forget to affirm your special person in public, but more importantly, believe in your spouse and let him/her know in private as well.

Words Focused on Character. The last principle we learn from Jesus' first encounter with Peter is that affirmation needs to focus on who we are, not just on what we do. When affirming Peter, Jesus could have focused just on what Peter would do. Can you hear how different the conversation would sound and feel? "You, Simon, will be an effective communicator or evangelist." Instead Jesus affirmed Peter's character and potential. "You are a rock." This volatile fisherman was told that in his character he was stable. I wonder what Peter thought when he heard these words? *Who me? No way. I've sure got Him fooled!* Or did he say, "The me You see is the me I want to be."

Each of us is significant and of great value in God's eyes because of what Jesus Christ accomplished on the cross, not because of what we accomplish. His love and affirmation are constant and unconditional.

Certainly each of us wants to be affirmed for what we do, but let's take it a step further. Let's affirm our mates for who they are: beautiful, sensitive, strong, faithful, and loving children of God.

We can both testify that when we find ourselves affirmed verbally, a transformation happens in us. It's as if we give each other not only acceptance but also confidence and strength. We end up saying, "He/she believes in me and what I can do. I've found out I can do more than I realized."

At the beginning of this chapter, we asked you to write down ten things you appreciate about your spouse. Before you read any further, we suggest you find your special someone. Tell him/her you are his/her number-one fan. Let him/her know specifically and directly the ten things you really appreciate.

One day we were listening to a tape produced by

Charlie and Martha Shedd. On it they mention that they try to give one another a new compliment every day. This is a fabulous goal. We have made it ours. Perhaps you would like to make it yours! Dr. Robert Schuller says:

> I must believe that I have value as a person! No matter who I am, I can be an encourager! I can be a spreader of hope! I can be a spirit-lifter to disheartened people! I can be a conduit, a channel for God's love, joy, and peace to flow to other human beings! I can love others and myself with God's love![5]

This, then, is the power of love. It's allowing yourself to be the channel of God's unconditional love and acceptance to the person you chose to marry. It is also speaking affirmations needed in his/her life because you feel the warmth of God's affirmations in your own heart.

6

Adding Sparkle to Your Marriage

FROM RIGID TO ROMANCER

A marriage is old when two people feel that there is nothing more to discover together. Since there is always something new to share, most of the marriages that grow old are the ones that allow themselves to grow old.

DR. DAVID VISCOTT [1]

How many elderly couples have you seen holding hands lately? It's a rare and welcome sight, isn't it. In a Christ-centered marriage it is not enough to have an attitude of appreciation about your special someone. It is not enough to speak words of affirmation, although love talk is crucial. If you truly want to serve your mate you must be willing, as Christ was, to act on your words. Because affirmation needs to be experienced by your spouse, we encourage you to recall the last time you planned a surprise for your mate just because you love him/her.

Unfortunately, there seems to be a rumor afloat that

such service to your spouse is wimpy. Some believe doing concrete romantic acts represents an adolescent mentality, and if it's true love, romance will just happen automatically. Nonsense! This kind of thinking causes one to be a selfish, passive responder in his/her marriage rather than a loving initiator. Passive responses place us constantly on the defensive and increase our feelings of anxiousness. They also increase our tendency to judge. It doesn't take long before we find ourselves comparing what our spouse is or isn't doing to what everyone else's mate is doing. What a useless waste of time! No one else has a perfect marriage because all marriages unite two imperfect individuals.

Making Romance a Priority

The belief that putting love into action is just for the adolescent demonstrates a real misunderstanding of love. Love takes constant tending and attention. It takes time and it takes overtime. You don't build a great marriage in the odd moments when you're not doing anything else. A great marriage takes much thought, prayer, creativity, planning, and ingenuity. It requires a willingness to study your mate so you can choose actions that delight rather than offend. A great relationship also requires lots of imagination, combined with a willingness to be the initiator. It only happens when a lover takes personal responsibility to serve his/her partner by making the marriage relationship interesting, fun, and alive.

Being romantic means treating your marriage as if it is important. Many couples believe that if they surround themselves with the externals of romance—if they sit in a glamorous restaurant with candlelight and music—something incredible will happen to their relationship.

Externals are great and can be very pleasant, but the

basis of romance happens within the mind of the individual man and woman. Do they treat their marriage as if it is top priority?

This understanding of romance is tremendously important to all of us but must be especially stressed *if this is not your first marriage.* Love can never be duplicated and to try is deadly. Reaching back for yesterday's happiness can sabotage today.

The two of you are facing many more relationships in your intimate circle than do couples who are getting married for the first time. Perhaps you may be joining two families—with all the resulting confusion. It is crucial in the midst of this change for you to make time on a daily basis for just the two of you—a time to reaffirm that your relationship is indeed top priority.

It has been said that when we marry, we exchange the attentions of many for the inattention of one. What a sad commentary on many modern marriages. You see, if both of you are committed to your marriage and to each other, you can mirror each other with positives. The more attentive you are to your spouse, the more he/she will be to you. The kinder you are to your spouse, the kinder he/she will be to you. The greater number of surprises you delight your spouse with, the happier you will be. And who knows—you just might end up surprised one day! We need a clear understanding in this self-centered society of ours that *how* our marriages are doing depends a whole lot on *what* we're doing. Love breeds love.

You must begin with a Christ-centered marriage. After all, it is the Holy Spirit, actively transforming each partner's will, who empowers us to be willing servants to our mates. Yet as we allow this transformation to take place in our minds and wills, we still have to acknowledge that love takes work. It's the most fun work in the world but it's still work.

Romancing Is Fun

The following ideas for adding sparkle to your marriage are a collection of Congo traditions and marvelous activities creative couples have shared with us. We gladly provide these activities which are designed to put love in action. They have enriched our marriage and the marriages of many other couples. Choose those activities that are compatible with both of your personalities. Great marriages must start somewhere. Why not with you?

1. Greet each other with affection when you come into the house after being away. Get out of your chair, stop what you are doing, and give each other a hug and a kiss. Welcome each other as you would Christ Himself. Remember, the first three minutes after you arrive home often sets the mood for the entire evening.

2. Plan a weekly date night. It needn't be expensive, but you do need to plan for a regular time alone together that includes face-to-face conversation. Make that night sacred. No matter how hectic your week is, give this night top priority. We have found it adds excitement when spouses alternate the planning.

3. Remember always to kiss each other good morning and good night. It takes such a little bit of effort but it pays huge dividends.

4. When was the last time you scheduled yourself into your spouse's office hours—using a phony name? If you can't remember, try it. Take along a favorite snack, a picnic lunch, or a special dessert. (After reading our list you'll notice we enjoy eating!)

5. Tuck notes in your spouse's purse, briefcase, underwear, suitcase, or wherever. Be wise and make sure his/her secretary doesn't discover one!

6. At the drugstore you can buy empty plastic capsules commonly used for drugs. Fill your capsules with love notes and leave these "marriage vitamins" everywhere.

7. Send balloons or a plant to work, thanking your spouse for last night. A little healthy embarrassment is good for any relationship.

8. Include money in your family budget for "just the two of you" activities. Those activities might include going to the beach, hiking in the mountains, playing a round of miniature golf, swimming, skating, watching a good movie, and so forth.

9. Emilie Barnes introduced us to the idea of a love basket and we wouldn't be without it. It is a large wicker basket complete with a cloth, napkins, utensils, goblets, and candles. It is to be used only by the two of you. It can be packed by the husband or wife. It's the perfect accessory for date nights, sick calls—your imagination is the limit. Our love basket has gone to the library, the beach, the park, a college campus, and of course, the office. Once it didn't go any farther than our bedroom, and that time was the best of all.

10. Show your love with plenty of cuddling, nuzzling, kissing, and hugging. We heard a California psychologist say that we all need four hugs a day to survive, eight to maintain, and twelve to thrive. He didn't say who should initiate the hugs. How are *you* doing?

11. Every marriage has to have childless moments. Family vacations are wonderful but they favor the family. Farm out the kids once in a while and plan a candlelight dinner. Purchase a new record or tape to remember the evening by. A couple we know decided to have a nude luau. Is that too radical for your tastes? If so, plan a dinner that is more your style. But whatever you do, have fun and be imaginative.

12. Have you forgotten how to flirt? If so, polish up your skills and practice just on your spouse at the next large gathering you attend.

13. Don't stop writing love letters after you marry. Use holidays as occasions to express your love in writing. Marriage Encounter suggests that you use this tool often, especially when something is so important to you that it's difficult to express verbally.

14. Find out when the moon will be full. Arrange for a baby-sitter and kidnap your spouse. Plan a midnight picnic. We'll leave the rest up to you.

15. Clip out notices in newspapers and magazines that you think will interest your spouse. One friend of ours loves bluegrass music and is taking banjo lessons. When his wife noticed an advertisement for a bluegrass concert in their local paper, she clipped it out, placed it in an envelope, and put it under his pillow. A couple of weeks later they enjoyed a date night together while listening to good music.

16. Give each other the gift of thirty minutes alone, every day, with no accountability for how it's spent.

17. Pray for your spouse. If you don't do it, who will? Before an important meeting, phone to let him/her know you're praying.

18. Plan a daily debriefing time. We have a daily teatime and because of our schedules, we meet at 10:00 P.M. We have friends who send their children to do homework while they linger at the table after dinner. Other friends find morning to be the best time. We also enjoy walking together and talking; do you? It doesn't matter when you do it, just do it. But beware. If you use this time to dump garbage on your spouse, don't be surprised if your relationship stinks. We guard our conversation during our teatime by including positive statements:

"I so appreciated you today when. . . ."
"I learned today. . . ."
"The most positive thing that happened to me
    today was. . . ."

19. Buy each other a favorite magazine or give a subscription if the funds allow.

20. Help your spouse reach a goal by leaving motivational notes around the house. Be his/her cheering squad.

21. Invest in sexy underwear—for yourself and your mate.

22. Buy or make a card or gift for no special reason.

23. Allow your mate some time with his/her friends. In fact, suggest that you get together with each other's friends.

24. Go out for breakfast together once in a while. It will give you a whole new perspective on your relationship. But we offer a warning: there are conflicting feelings about this suggestion!

Anne Morrow Lindbergh wrote these words: "It's a simple enough pleasure, surely, to have breakfast alone with one's husband, but how seldom married people in the midst of life achieve it."[2]

Winston Churchill wrote: "My wife and I tried to breakfast together, but we had to stop or our marriage would have been wrecked."[3] Since he and Mrs. Churchill are known to have had a great marriage, one of them must not have been a morning person!

You be the judge. We love sharing breakfast together.

25. Learn to say *no* to social activities that seem to be interfering with quality couple time. Be especially mindful during the holiday seasons.

26. Run a bubble bath for your spouse complete with candlelight and a favorite musical tape. (Option: Get in!)

27. Buy your spouse a mug, trophy, or plaque which proclaims him/her as the world's best roommate, husband, wife, and so forth.

28. If your spouse is under a great deal of pressure, answer the phone for him/her. Take down important information so the call can be returned later. Add icing on the cake by doing one of his/her chores without making a big deal about it.

29. When your mate tells a joke, determine not to help, roll your eyes in disbelief, or give away the punch line.

30. Invite your spouse out to lunch, and afterward suggest a motel. Even if there is no time, your spouse will love you for the idea.

31. Allow your mate to have separate interests. But beware. These can bring you together or drive you apart. Make a concentrated effort to bring separate interests back into marriage to enrich it. Practice being two, not just one.

Sheldon Vanauken writes in his book *A Severe Mercy:* "If one of us likes anything, there must be something to like in it and the other must find it. . . . That way we create a thousand strands great and small that will link us together. . . . And our trust in each other will not only be based on love and loyalty, but on the fact of a thousand sharings, a thousand strands twisted into something unbreakable."[4]

32. Take up a hobby together, choosing anything you will both enjoy. Are you drawing a blank? Then consider tennis, sailing, golfing, walking, running, reading, camping, cooking, gardening, collecting, bowling, swimming, racquetball, bicycling, bird-watching, woodworking, or attending sports events.

33. Plan an "I love my husband/wife" party. Make it a total surprise, including his/her dearest friends.

34. Make a tape-recorded love letter for your mate.

35. Send a telegram to work, inviting your mate to a weekend away. Make all the arrangements yourself, including the packing.

36. A darling pastor and his wife in their sixties noticed that nobody thinks anything of hugging and kissing in an airport, so they came up with a plan. Whenever they're close to an airport he lets her off at one door, drives his car to the far door, and parks. They walk toward the middle and whoever sees the other first starts running. They both run and hug as if

they haven't seen one another in ages. They have a list of all the airports in which they've hugged. We think they're great.

37. Thank each other for the little things. Don't take your spouse for granted as one woman did: "My working wife had no more vacation time, though I had some. Bored with being home alone, I decided to surprise her by doing the dishes, cleaning the basement, and doing other assorted chores. When she came home that night I expected to be praised for my efforts, but she said nothing. Finally I said, "Didn't you even notice all the things I did around the house today?"

With a sigh, she said, "Yeah, it's a thankless job, isn't it?"[5]

38. Set aside time weekly to evaluate your relationship. Our time is Sunday evening, after the children are put to bed. We check one another's schedules for the next week. We discuss them and pray over them. Next we check our priorities. Are we living by them? Then we review last week. How did we do as a husband/wife team?

39. Charlie Shedd writes that when he and his wife Martha have houseguests they leave this note on a plate of Danish rolls:

> Whenever we have overnight company, we have a compact that we will go out for breakfast alone. Thanks for coming.[6]

Wow! It depends on your company, we guess. We're still thinking this one through.

40. Praise each other often, when the other is—and isn't—within earshot.

41. Exchange foot massages and back rubs.

42. Read the same chapter of a book, previously chosen by the two of you, during the week. While on your date night discuss the thoughts that really hit you. We would like to recommend you begin with a book discussing marriage or relationships.

43. Last thing at night or after your morning kiss, pray aloud together about your marriage. Express your love for each other and your thankfulness for God's goodness to you.

44. Create your own language. Suggestions:

> Y.S.S. = You're so sexy.
> C.Y.K. = Consider yourself kissed.
> H.G.L. = Hey, good lookin'!

45. Little things can mean so much. Does he have a weakness for lemon meringue pie? Surprise him with it occasionally. Does she have a special fragrance? Surprise her.

46. One dear couple didn't have any money for Christmas one year. He was quite nervous because under the tree there was a beautifully wrapped gift with his name on it. He opened it to find lots of brightly colored tissue paper and a note. It read: THIS BOX CONTAINS ALL MY LOVE FOR YOU. ANYTIME YOU ARE FEELING LONELY, OVERWHELMED, OR JUST DOWN, PLEASE OPEN THIS BOX AND KNOW THAT I LOVE YOU. Being a together hubby, he took the box to work and put it on his desk. Many businessmen asked him what it was. He told them. As a result several of them came to know the Lord.

47. Wear the clothes or colognes, eat the chocolates, and smell the flowers your spouse gives you—

even if you might not have chosen them yourself. (One chocolate won't ruin your diet!)

48. Dash home at the noon hour for a "quickie" that will send you both back to work with smiles on your faces.

49. Let your mate sleep ten minutes more while you make the coffee.

50. When the time is right, tell your mate that you'd happily marry him/her all over again.

If you haven't tried even one of these since you were married, perhaps your mate is still with you only because he/she is a Christian. If you've tried some that we haven't mentioned, please write us and let us know what they are. We're always on the lookout for new ways to put love into action.[7]

Love in action takes time, willpower, imagination, and knowledge of your mate. The willingness to be the initiator of affirmation in your thought life, through your choice of words and through your actions, takes effort. As you become a willing and loving servant to your mate, there will be an interesting result: Your own feelings of self-love will grow, as will your love for the person you married.

Silver Donald Cameron, a Canadian writer, puts it this way:

I do not know firsthand what the right man does for a woman, but I do know what the right woman does for a man. The woman you marry makes you feel capable, not captured. She makes you feel bigger, stronger, and more enabled than you ever were without her. She becomes a friend so special that the world seems pallid and bland without her. . . . No matter how stupid and weak you may have been, you cannot be wholly rotten, because she is no fool, and she loves you.

A woman who strengthens and enhances you, who loves you both for your strengths and weaknesses, who tolerates your contradictions and ambiguities, a woman who loves *you*—such a woman evokes a devotion that is perpetually fresh and vital. She makes you feel like a finer person than you thought you were. Feeling that way, you act that way; you achieve the best that is in you. You grow, and you grow together.

A man could no more leave such a woman than he could divorce his lungs or his eyesight. Such a woman is not just a lover, not even just a mate. She is the other half of himself, and with her he is, at last, complete.[8]

7

Do I Dare to Be Real?

FROM VEILED TO VULNERABLE

*The idea of spending time together in
intimate situations is foreign to an awful lot
of people. Instead of talking, we all watch HBO.
Our culture is so permeated with the notion
that sex is the answer to loneliness that sex
has replaced true intimacy.*

RICHARD BOSCH [1]

Buried in our urge to marry we find the need for security. It is our desire to matter most to someone and to be loved by someone as we truly are. We often fantasize before marriage about hours spent together, looking into one another's eyes, into one another's very souls, and being delighted with the wonder we find.

Then something happens. It's as if the cares of this world rise up and choke our dreams. The floor of Dave's office has literally been drenched by the tears of marital partners who have been dying to be heard by the most important person in their lives. The agonizing cry is the same: "We just don't communicate anymore."

They do not talk much anymore, but never does a couple stop communicating. "Anthropologist Ray Birdwhistell equipped one hundred couples with microphones to determine how much conversation goes on between them during the course of a week. He eliminated all grunts, all simple announcements like 'Dinner is on the table' and such minimal replies as 'Yes, dear' and came up with a grand total of twenty-eight minutes a week [of conversation]."[2] That's a sad commentary on our talking time, but talking is not to be confused with communicating. We are always communicating with our body language, facial expressions, gestures, mannerisms, and even silence.

An interdependent marriage is a journey of mutual discovery. Each of us is in the process of being transformed from day-to-day, moment to moment. The same is true of our mates. The question facing each married person is, *Am I going to close myself off from this "stranger" until I am certain our relationship is safe, or am I going to begin the process of discovering who this person is and revealing to him/her who I am?* If you risk communicating, your mate, even a stranger, becomes known to you and in the process you learn more about yourself. Leo Buscaglia puts it well:

> To live in love is life's greatest challenge. It requires more subtlety, flexibility, sensitivity, understanding, acceptance, tolerance, knowledge and strength than any other human endeavor or emotion. . . .[3]

People are always changing; is the hope of communicating an unrealistic one? No. This very truth keeps our marriage relationships fascinating and unpredictable. One evening you share a beautiful, candlelight, romantic dinner together, and the next morning at 2:00 A.M. your wife falls in the toilet because you left the seat up. The work of keeping in touch with each other, of discovering and willingly discarding expectations, goes on through the entire lifetime of a marriage. But there is no such thing as instant success in this area of communication.

Head Talk and Heart Talk

More often than we would care to enumerate we run into couples who just take turns talking. How lonely they are, and how cruel is that loneliness.

Even though we don't want to admit it when we're dating, marriage is a package deal. We don't just marry our spouse, we also marry his/her family. How did your mate's family communicate? What did you learn about communicating in your own home? Please pause and think through those two questions before reading on. Did you hear many words, but no real intimate communication? Did you hear cold silence or did you hear love spoken there? Your answers determine whether you are working on your Ph.D. or enrolled in preschool as far as your communications skills are concerned. Anne Ortlund writes:

> The more different your backgrounds and your previous cultures and points of view, the more you'll misunderstand each other. But *understand that you'll misunderstand*, and don't give up.[4]

Before marriage your biggest decision was what to do on Saturday evening, who would be in your wedding party, and where you would spend your honeymoon. After the wedding you deal with the nitty-gritty of finances, home location, children, job responsibilities, and sexual adjustments—just to mention a few.

We've also been brainwashed by our society to believe that in order for love to be real, it must be spontaneous. Unfortunately in our day and age, love expressed through words must be scheduled or it just won't happen. So many things demand our attention that it is easy to give communication a low priority. For this reason, as mentioned before, we highly suggest a date night each week and a coffee time each day. Our marriage has been enriched by these times.

Somehow communicating with our mates has taken on serious, somber, and negative overtones. That's why each marriage needs "head talk" and "heart talk" times.

Head talk is just the day-to-day sharing of reality. It's the fun of communicating about things that aren't earth-shattering, just interesting. *Heart talk* is the willingness to be vulnerable, the sharing of feelings and beliefs that are tremendously important to both of you.

Every relationship needs balance. If you have unrealistic expectations that all your conversations will be heart-to-heart times, your relationship will be much too intense. If, on the other hand, all your communication is superficial head talk, that is frustrating as well.

Perhaps you are feeling alone because you and your spouse really haven't been having either head or heart sessions. How can you get his/her attention? You've got to begin talking his/her language.

The story is told of a lady who came to a marriage counselor because she had decided she wanted to divorce her husband. The counselor, wanting to save the marriage, asked her a few preliminary questions to see if he couldn't locate and solve the problem.

First he asked, "Do you have any grounds?"

She answered, "Yes, we have about an acre."

"That's not exactly what I mean. I mean, do you have a grudge?"

"No," came the reply. "We have a carport."

Trying a third time, the counselor asked, "Does he beat you up?"

"No, I'm always up before he is."

"Well, then, why do you want to divorce your husband?" the frustrated counselor asked.

"Because you can't carry on an intelligent conversation with him."

What are your mate's interests? What is dear to his/her heart? If you haven't been communicating on a regular basis, don't expect to be involved in a heart-to-heart session. No way! What you both need is some fun and some talk. Learn something new about your mate.

Dr. Robert Anthony has placed in order of importance the things people enjoy talking about. It is an illuminating list.

1. Their interests
2. Their opinions
3. Other people
4. Things in general
5. You[5]

Have your conversations gotten self-centered?

Perhaps you have been using the first person singular pronoun with increasing frequency. Not for one moment are we saying that the personal pronoun is destructive to all communication. It is the tool necessary for heart-to-heart times. However, it is not the tool for head times. Head times need to focus on learning all you can about your partner and what makes him/her tick. It is your time to ask all kinds of questions and to be a fascinated listener. Enjoy your special someone.

Do you use your partner only as a form of cheap therapy, a dumping station for all your problems? Some marriage partners aren't grown-ups, they're groan-ups! Conversation time with their spouses is only a license for complaining about him/her, their kids, their jobs, and their friends. Then they're amazed that this same spouse doesn't want to take the time to talk. Watch yourself and watch your conversations.

If petty annoyances are dragging you down, don't blame your partner. Do something to cheer yourself up. Putting your happiness totally in your spouse's hands keeps you forever dependent, critical, and judgmental.

A marriage not only needs the balance of head and heart times, it also needs the balance of grace and truth.

Grace and Truth

We need to be one another's mutual admiration society. Sixty newlyweds were interviewed for their complaints. Do you know that the men's major complaint was that there was not enough verbal expression of affection on the part of their wives?[6] We need to be willing to be affirmers in our partners' lives. We must be willing servants, bringing grace to our husbands/wives. Let your special person know that he/she is precious to you.

In Ephesians 4:15 Paul tells us to "speak the truth in love." That's the balance. Constructive honesty builds up. Destructive honesty tears down. Sensitive speakers are needed. One author made this point rather sarcastically:

> The Bible tells us that Samson killed ten thousand Philistines with the jawbone of an ass. I am convinced that an even greater number of conversations are killed daily with the same instrument.[7]

Be courteous in all your communication with your spouse. Marriage does not give you license for rudeness.

**Balance
head talk
with
heart talk.
Balance
grace with truth.**

Words cause a permanent imprint. Martin Buber defines a true dialogue as one in which the speaker has the other person's individuality and special needs in mind. Loving dialogue is accepting, understanding, and empathetic.

The words you use tell so much about you. The way you express yourself is an outward manifestation of your inner attitude. Research confirms that in face-to-face conversations, 7 percent of a message depends on the words, 23 percent on the tone of voice, and 70 percent on nonverbal body language.[8] Do you demonstrate love and grace in your choice of words, your tone of voice, and your body language? To increase your awareness of the type of communicator you would like to be, answer these questions:

1. How would you describe a great communicator? (Take into account these factors: body language, eyes, and voice.)
2. How does he/she listen?
3. How does he/she let the partner know he/she is being heard?
4. How does he/she make the spouse feel comfortable?
5. What kinds of questions might he/she ask?

Do *you* talk in such a way that your spouse will be glad he/she listened? If so, your conversations are characterized by grace.

Is your communication equally characterized by truth? Love is not the same as mental telepathy. Our mates are not mind readers. Don't expect your husband/wife to know what you're upset about—tell him/her. There is nothing so bad that it cannot be made even worse by stewing about it.

If you want something, say so. Don't give him/her two

options if you really want one. Game playing is not part of a Christ-centered partnership. We have to get honest with each other. Confront one another in love if one of you is preoccupied. "Hey, honey, I know you're in there. I need to know what you're thinking." Don't hope your wife won't object if you bring guests home for dinner. Give her a phone call and get her perspective.

If you're feeling neglected, say so. Perhaps all he's been talking about lately is his work. Share some interesting things that have been happening to you. If you're both happy, busy, and confident, your conversations will be more fun. If one of you goes through a hard time, it will affect both of you. Please don't exaggerate. If your spouse is in a rotten mood, it doesn't mean that you've got a rotten marriage.

The tool for communicating honestly is *I* statements. Using the word *I* and following it with a descriptive verb such as, "*I feel frustrated . . . I need . . . I hope . . . I perceive the situation differently . . . I won't. . . .*" The beauty of this discipline is that it keeps us from attacking, blaming, or scapegoating our partners. As long as we use *I* statements, we stay honest and interdependent.

Perhaps you were raised to believe that saying *I* is selfish. Perhaps you've accepted this philosophy so long you don't even know what you want. The following exercise may feel uncomfortable and strange. That's a natural reaction to something different. Anything new feels uncomfortable, not necessarily because it's wrong but because it's unfamiliar. Persist prayerfully and answer these questions honestly:

1. I want _____ from my marriage.

2. I need _____ from my spouse.

MY COMMUNICATION COVENANT
WITH MY SPOUSE

I will tell you often that I love you.

I will tell others what a special person you are to me.

I will talk to you politely.

I will initiate compliments and affirmations.

I will affirm your character when you've succeeded and failed.

I will accept your perceptions as legitimate ones.

I will enjoy your uniqueness.

I will show my love for you in little ways you will appreciate.

I will make time for head-to-head times.

I will make time for heart-to-heart times.

I will celebrate our relationship daily with a kiss, a prayer, a smile, and a loving word.

I will incorporate silliness into our adult relationship.

I will touch you, hug you, and hold you just because I love you.

I will tell you when I need you.

I will allow you moments of quietness and separateness. It will enrich you emotionally and spiritually, and therefore it will enrich our relationship.

I will laugh with you on a daily basis.

I will listen to you without preoccupation, judgment, or criticism.

I will listen to your feelings as well as your thoughts.

I will be honest with you.

I will be gentle with you.

I will continue to work at understanding myself.

I will open up my world to you.

I will be flexible and acknowledge our marriage as an ever-changing reality.

I will grow up separately together with you.

I will keep your confidence.

I will express gratitude when you have opened your soul to me.

I will be loyal to you.

I will respect you and your perspective.

I will be your friend.

Throughout this book we have been suggesting that you be God's servant to your spouse. Some understand servanthood to mean they must do whatever their spouse asks of them. We think that would be harmful. You are an obedient servant to Christ, *not* a servant to your partner's whims when they are evil. Speaking the truth in love means discerning and saying what is really in your spouse's best interest. There is an enormous difference between what sounds good and what is good. What is good is constructive honesty. Often speaking what sounds good can be dishonest.

Has your relationship been all head talk lately? Perhaps you have a major decision to make or something is bothering you. This is the time to honestly look your mate in the eyes and to request a heart-to-heart time. Suggest an agreed-upon place and a convenient time. Then come prepared with *I* statements and with lots of grace. If you are verbalizing frustrations, don't forget the affirmations. Likewise, continually ask yourself these questions:

1. Am I making myself clear, using *I* statements?
2. Do I have a hidden message?
3. How am I making my spouse feel?
4. What tone is my voice conveying?
5. How do I look as I say this?

Recognizing Your Partner's Fears

Because of the home he/she was raised in, because of hurts from past relationships, or for any number of reasons, your spouse may be terrified of heart-to-heart times. You will never convince him/her that opening up is important to your marriage by calling him/her insensitive, a workaholic, frigid, or by attacking his/her parents. Love and acceptance are the only attitudes that will break down the walls. Make these phrases a part of your conversations:

"I love you."
"I miss talking together."
"Why don't we spend an intimate evening together on Monday. I'll plan something special."

Each spouse needs to be aware that when he doesn't share who he is because of the fear of rejection, when she is afraid to voice her opinion because of failing to meet her spouse's expectations, when he hides what he is feeling from himself, and when she will only receive love given in the way that fits her expectations, love and intimacy are blocked. When we are afraid of being too emotional or afraid of appearing stupid in our partners' eyes, we often hold back. Then we become strangers to both our spouses and ourselves. Real love is dedicated to a continual ''becoming.''

We must be aware that silence talks. It may speak the language of empathy or understanding, or it may tell of withdrawal and anger. It isn't always silence that bothers our loved ones. It's silence about emotions, feelings, love, and appreciation.

One day a heartbroken woman sat in Dave's office and said, ''I never know what he's thinking. I feel left out of his life.'' Her husband was afraid that she would leave him when she saw how insecure he was feeling, so he didn't open up to her. The sad fact was, she didn't know what he was thinking and she *was* ready to leave him.

We naturally assume that if we let our spouses see our weaknesses, they won't like us. This logic is as old as Adam and Eve. When they disobeyed God, they put a protective covering over themselves. They were attempting to hide.

If you want your spouse to know you, *you must communicate yourself to him/her.* Contrary to your worst fantasies of rejection, it helps your spouse feel close to you. Often he/she is more lenient with you than you are with yourself. Communicating honestly will also help you to hear your own voice, to awaken yourself to your resources, and to make your own choices within the context of a supportive relationship. You will discover more about yourself.

But we have a warning for you. If you lovingly encourage your mate to reveal his/her inner feelings, you must not make him/her regret the decision. You must learn to keep secrets. You can't tell mutual friends. You must never use it as evidence against him/her in the next conflict. You have been given a sacred trust.

Sometimes the more we need love, the more unlovely

and self-protective we become. The higher the walls we build between each other, the less our chances of finding love.

Dr. David Seamands shares about the freedom that vulnerability brought to his and his wife's relationship.

We were in India, and through a converging of nationalism, Hinduism, and communism, we *had* to leave a certain area just as I was drowning in my own successes. We were at the heart of a mass movement; I was baptizing three thousand new believers a year—a rare privilege for a young man in his late twenties. We were building a new church every month. I had said, "This is my dream; we're going to stay here a lifetime." It was a miniature Pentecost.

But God knew better. I would have been the biggest phony in the world if we had stayed there. When we were forced out, I really hit bottom.

Until then, my wife had always seemed a bit on the weepy side, and so I had thought, *My goodness—if I tell her what's bugging me about the church or the mission station—that it's getting to the lonely, scared boy inside of me—we'll go down the tube together. I don't dare tell her.* I felt I had to play the strong role.

Actually, she *wasn't* weak; she was just expressive. The moment I revealed my weakness, the most amazing thing happened. She said, "My goodness— I never knew whether you needed me." Suddenly she opened up like a flower to the sun and became the strong person she had always been. I only had to let her know she was needed. I allowed her to minister to me.[9]

Christ brought that balance into our lives. "For the law was given through Moses; grace and truth came through Jesus Christ" (John 1:17). As God's love connection to our spouses, do we dare convenant to be the bearers of truth and grace? If we risk, we will experience the power of love.

I want what I say to stimulate you, to bring you peace, to help you grow to your ultimate potential. I want what I say to bring us totally together. You have dignity and therefore my interaction with you must offer you all that you deserve, the *total me* at the moment.[10]

COMMUNICATION STYLES

Dependent	*Independent*	*Interdependent*
Communicates to understand you better.	Communicates to understand me better.	Communicates to understand each of us better.
Often head talk.	Often head talk.	A balance of head and heart talk.
Grace talk.	Truth talk.	A balance of grace and truth talk.
Refuses to be vulnerable (fears rejection).	Uncomfortable being vulnerable (fears rejection).	Risks being vulnerable (affirms acceptance).
Repeats pain (dishonest).	Inflicts pain with words (destructive honesty).	Expresses hurt and relieves pain (constructive honesty).
Uses *you* and *I* statements.	Uses *you* and *I* statements.	Uses *I* statements.
Silence of anger and withdrawal. Compliance.	Silence of anger and withdrawal.	Silence of empathy and understanding.

8

Does Anybody Care?

FROM CLONE TO COMPANION

*Listen to me for a day . . . an hour . . .
a moment! lest I expire in my terrible
wilderness, my lonely silence! O God, is
there no one to listen?*

SENECA 4 B.C.

Paul Tillich has said that the first duty of love is to *listen*. The way we listen has a much greater impact on our mate's self-esteem than does the way we talk. Each of us is terribly threatened by indifference. The opposite of love is not hate; it is indifference.

Listening Communicates Love

Concentrated listening tells your mate he/she is important to you, as are his/her ideas, feelings, and problems. It conveys respect and dignity. It is a means of modeling God's love. "I waited patiently for the Lord; and he inclined unto me, and heard my cry" (Psalms 40:1 KJV).

Active listening is the number-one way wives can obey Ephesians 5:33 (AMPLIFIED):

However, let each man of you (without exception) love his wife as [being in a sense] his very own self; and let the wife see that she respects *and* reverences her husband—that she notices him, regards him, honors him, prefers him, venerates and esteems him; and that she defers to him, praises him, and loves and admires him exceedingly.

Listening is one of the most precious ways wives can love their husbands.

Concentrating on your spouse's words helps you step out of your selfishness. Don't spend a lifetime trying to turn your mate into a clone—you won't be happy with your creation. When you reject this tendency, you will understand yourself and your spouse better.

Perhaps these are just a few reasons James 1:19 says, ". . . be quick to listen, slow to speak and slow to become angry." Then in Proverbs 18:13 we read:

> He who answers before listening—
> that is his folly and his shame.

How do you listen? Do you give out signals of irritation, boredom, or sarcasm? Do you thoughtlessly attack your mate's words or ignore both the words and feelings behind the words? If any of these reactions are habitual for you, there is no question in our minds but that your spouse is feeling personally rejected.

One anonymous writer put his feelings on paper:

> When I ask you to listen to me
> and you start giving advice,
> You have not done what I asked.

When I ask you to listen to me
  and you begin to tell me why
  I shouldn't feel that way,
You are trampling on my feelings.

When I ask you to listen to me
  and you feel you have to do
  something to solve my problems,
You have failed me,
strange
as that may seem. . . .

So please, just listen and hear me.
And if you want to talk,
  wait a few moments for your turn
  and I promise I'll listen to you.

Listening Communicates Acceptance

To be a great listener, you've got to want to be one. You must say *yes* to differences. You must also be willing to drop your preconceived notions about your spouse. To listen well is to care about your spouse's feelings as much as you do your own. It is to acknowledge that there are no boring spouses, only disinterested listeners. It is to affirm that fast advice often addresses a false problem. When you are a great listener your special someone will feel Christ's unconditional acceptance through you. Is your mate starving for acceptance?

Dr. Carl Rogers points out that "the major barrier to mutual interpersonal communication is our very natural tendency to judge, to evaluate, to approve or disapprove the statement of the other person. . . ."[1] When you draw your mate out by asking interesting and probing questions and react with negativity, judgment, and condemnation, you will shut the door to future communication. If this is your weak area, please memorize this sentence. Practice it over and over in front of a mirror, ask your mate a question, take a deep breath, smile, and use this line:

"I didn't realize such things bothered you."

This statement keeps you from being on the defensive, and it doesn't slam the door to future communication.

As we said before, couples spend so much time talking but so little time communicating. What would happen to your relationship if you couldn't speak for three months? How would you feel? Would this experience bring you face-to-face with the fact that you and your mate have never really confided your inner feelings, your hopes, and your dreams? What would you do?

This nightmare happened to Rhea Zakich, the creator of the Ungame. As a method of coping with her inability to speak because of a problem with her vocal cords, she sat at her kitchen table one evening with a stack of blank cards to create a game. On each card she wrote a question—some serious and some lighthearted. There was only one rule: nobody was to talk out of turn. This game had no winners or losers and encouraged only sharing and communicating.

Her family played the game at the dinner table the next evening, with Rhea writing down her answers. The first fact she learned about her husband was that he had fears. She hadn't stopped talking long enough to hear that before—and so it went. In *Reader's Digest* Rhea wrote, "Silence taught me that the listener is the most important person in any conversation."[2]

Listening is an investment in your spouse's life. It is a way of saying to your mate, "You are not alone. I am here with you."

Listening Aided by Feedback

When real understanding is desired, feedback is essential. It is never safe to assume that the message received is the same as the sender intended. We usually make the assumption that our judgments are right. They aren't necessarily! We know you believe you understand what you think we said, but we're not sure you realize that what you heard is not what we meant. Confused? We all need to incorporate feedback.

But what is feedback? It is repeating, in your own words, what you heard your partner say and the feelings that you perceived were lying underneath the words. There are to be no judgments, no evaluations, and no opinions. Feedback is the process of coming alongside your mate. It puts your special person in touch with his/her own feelings.

The most effective feedback takes into account not only your spouse's words but also the tone of his/her voice, facial expression, posture, other body language, and silence. The purpose of feedback is to check out the perception of the world as it looks and feels to your mate. It is not enough just to be present.

> To be with you and to be dead is not
> renewing.
> To be with you reluctantly, resentfully,
> distractedly is not renewing.
> To be there for you is renewing when the
> message you get from my being there is
> that I want to be there, with you, be-
> cause I value you, and that I express
> that value by making an affirmative
> choice to be with you from all my
> choices.

> And having chosen to be with you, I give
> quality to our time together and to my
> presence with you by giving you my focus,
> my attention, in ways that give you mes-
> sages that you can translate into self-
> esteem.[3]

Usually the more important the message you are trying to get across to your mate, the greater the danger of misunderstanding. It is during these heart-to-heart times that feedback is crucial. These steps can further both of your goals and manipulation will be nonexistent if you use them.

Step 1:
Clearly express to your mate your desire for a heart-to-heart time. Check that the timing is right for both of you. Arrange a nonthreatening place to discuss this mutual concern. If something affects one partner, then it very naturally affects both. Perhaps you need to leave the house and get a cup of coffee at a restaurant if your tendency is to raise your voice and berate your mate, instead of sticking to the issue.

Step 2:
As clearly and simply as possible, describe the cause of concern using *I* statements. If you are having trouble defining what you are feeling, try checking this list:

hurt	inferior	tense
humiliated	silly	loved
lonely	jealous	rejected
intimidated	sympathy	disappointed
hatred	accepted	frustrated

hated	protective	impatient
confident	angry	superior
shy	sad	ashamed
useless	cheated	trapped
jubilant	unworthy	despair[4]

Speak no more than thirty seconds. Then ask your mate what he/she heard you say.

Step 3:
   A. Ask your spouse to paraphrase as accurately as possible (that is, feedback) what he/she heard you say.
   B. Feedback how he/she perceived you were feeling as you said it.
   C. Feedback how your words and feelings made him/her feel.

Step 4:
Either you acknowledge that your partner indeed got the message or you need to clarify the message. Then ask him/her to feedback to you what you said.

At first you will feel clumsy using the four steps involved in feedback. But we can guarantee that, used over time, they will revolutionize your communication. This process of listening with acceptance will help your mate feel great just because he/she is really being listened to. It helps him/her send a clear message. It will help you to understand and accept the individuality of your spouse at the same time that it will bring you together. You will feel as if you are a caring, loving, understanding mate, and your partner will feel validated. It sure beats manipulation.

We all need to enlarge our capacities to understand our mates' perspective, to be aware of their feelings, and to desire to do what we can to help. Sometimes the most helpful thing we can do is to listen. Through the act of listening to pain we give the opportunity to experience, assimilate, and eventually to be free of that pain. Beware of the repetition of pain as an excuse for inactivity or as a justification on your spouse's part for a martyr complex. If you sense either of these responses, it is time to feedback with great clarity how that makes you feel. Active listening doesn't only empathize, it also challenges the one listened to to grow.

Practice imagining how you would feel if you were in your spouse's situation or if you were looking at the world from your spouse's perspective. That is the skill of feedback. Even when you feel that you are most empathetic, resist the urge to tell your spouse that you know exactly what he/she is feeling. Chances are you don't.

Listening Aided by Separateness

Balance your growth in this area with an ever-increasing awareness of your separateness. If you don't, you will find your moods mirror your spouse's. When he/she is in the pits you are too. When this occurs, you can be of absolutely no help to him/her.

What if My Mate Is Suffering?

How do you respond when your mate is suffering? Complete this sentence: When I see my husband/wife suffering I. . . . No doubt you have many responses. Why don't you ask your spouse to tell you which of your responses are helpful and which are not.

If you are married to a person who falls apart every time you express pain, perhaps this question will help him/her understand your reaction: *How would you feel if I fell apart every time you expressed pain?* Listen actively with acceptance and feedback to his/her response. This is your chance to be a mirror.

What if My Mate Is Fearful?

Sentence completions can be tremendously helpful if you are married to a person who is very afraid of expressing emotions. Perhaps as a child or as an adult he was harshly ridiculed for any display of emotion. Your mate's response was to turn emotions off completely. How tragic, for he has denied himself self-understanding and you a major portion of himself. (This, of course, applies to women as well.)

If there is one silent partner in the relationship it is usually a couple problem. Our recommendation is that you both set aside time to talk. Begin by completing these sentences:

One of the ways I make it difficult for you to express your feelings is. . . .

One of the ways you can help me talk about my feelings is. . . .

Don't stop at one answer to the preceding statements. Force yourself to come up with five or maybe more. But remember this: if you really want your partner to talk about his/her feelings, you must accept what you hear. Remember the response you memorized early in the chapter?

I didn't realize such things bothered you.

Perhaps this is the time to use it!

To
listen well
is
to care
about your spouse's feelings
as much
as you do your own.

What if My Mate Criticizes Me?

This brings up the issue of criticism. Criticism is an evidence of intimacy's presence—not its absence. It has been said that infatuation blinds you to your mate's faults, while intimacy can lead one to see more faults than are actually there. How do you handle your mate's criticism of you? Do all your listening skills go out the window at this point?

You are dealing with a remnant from your childhood if you always feel attacked, always get angry or depressed, or if you always have to do what others disapprove of in order to prove yourself.

Don't lash out and attack your spouse. That will be your natural tendency. This is not a game of win and lose. This is either double win or double lose. You need to face the issue at hand together rather than arguing over who is "right."

Consider the criticism carefully, using your feedback skills to clarify your understanding of your mate's perspective. Don't cave in at the first raised eyebrow because you're afraid you can't live without your spouse's approval. Repeat and paraphrase what's just been said to you. This will validate both you and your partner.

Ask questions and get specific reasons for his/her disapproval. It may be that you are coming at the same issue from different perspectives. Always ask your mate for specific solutions. Keep making this a "we are together facing something that is irritating one of us" situation. There are times to give in. Obviously one is when your spouse has a good point. Perhaps you will also choose to give in when the issue doesn't matter a great deal to you but is tremendously important to your spouse.

In the midst of this discussion be honest. *I* statements are tremendously important to you. One woman put it this way: "I feel like a walking mistake when I'm constantly told that I do things wrong." Let your mate know you value him/her. If the criticism is unfair, say so and acknowledge it as your spouse's problem. Take it to the Lord, leave it with Him, and then give yourself permission to go on in spite of the very natural feelings of anxiety you will take with you.

What if a Change Is Needed?

If you decide that a change is necessary, set a goal together. Next, break it down into small "chewable" steps; pray over it; enlist your spouse as your cheering section. Growing apart is natural. Growing together takes hard work, but we're here to tell you it's worth it.

If you are interested in becoming an accepting listener, why not ask these questions when the time is right. Then use feedback to clarify if you received the message he/she sent.

What five things do you most want from
our marriage?
What needs do you have that I can help
you meet?
How can I set you free to be all that
you feel God wants you to be?
When do you feel that I am a good
listener or a poor listener?

It is also necessary to check your own progress. We have created a tool to help you and it is called a Communication Checkup.

COMMUNICATION CHECKUP

Each partner is to go through this questionnaire individually and score it himself/herself. Discuss your choices and why.

1 = All the time
2 = Most of the time
3 = Some of the time
4 = None of the time

Do I willingly set aside time to talk?

Am I feeling that both of us are important to this relationship?

When I disagree, can I stay on the issue?

Am I open to discussion of our relationship?

Do I use *I* statements?

Do I yell and talk too loudly?

Am I always giving my mate orders?

Am I sarcastic to my mate?

Do I affirm my mate in public?

Do I talk only about myself?

Do I try to see my mate's point of view?

Am I dogmatic, condescending, argumentative, or egocentric?

Do I monopolize our conversations?

Do I express my thoughts?

Do I try to make my mate feel guilty?

Do I withdraw in the midst of conflict?

Do I seek out my mate's opinions?

Do I affirm my mate honestly, consistently, and directly?

Do I affirm my mate as "in process"?

Do I use jealousy to get my mate's attention?

Do I sound insecure?

Do I speak the truth in love?

Do I accept myself as "in process"?

Do I accept my mate as a separate person?

Do I interrupt my mate when he/she is talking?

Do I get upset and defensive when my mate disagrees with me?

Am I often preoccupied when my mate is talking?

Am I able and willing to express clearly what I am thinking?

Do I share my feelings?

Do I talk longer than a minute without giving my spouse a chance to respond?

Do I exaggerate when upset?

Am I comfortable when we disagree?

Do I practice feedback with my mate?

Do I avoid accusations, ridicule, and name calling?

Do I tend to get "historical" when I am angry?

Do I take things too seriously?

When my mate criticizes me, do I feel defensive and try to fight back?

Do I feel that I am responsible for my mate?

Do I take personal responsibility for my own growth?

Do I pause a few moments to formulate my words before responding to my mate?

Am I an interested listener?

Do we have a good balance between head talk and heart talk in our relationship?

Do I insist on having the last word?

Do I have a well-developed sense of humor?

Am I kind?

Does my conversation have a balance of truth and grace?

Do I have difficulty admitting that I made a mistake?

Do I analyze my mate's character?

Do I overuse the words *always, never,* and *every time*?

Do I preach at my mate?

Do I shut the door to further communication with
    statements such as, "That's your problem" or "I
    don't want to hear anything about it"?
Do I foresee change in myself?
Do I foresee change in my mate?

You certainly won't have all the skills mastered—we
don't. That is not the point. The questions you should be
asking yourself are, *Am I progressing in the right direction?*
Am I more understanding, a clearer communicator, and a more
interested listener than I was two months ago?
We want to remind you that your actions can be as
important as your words. What you are speaks so loudly,
I can't hear what you are saying! Rhea Zakich tells a story
well worth repeating:

One evening, I played the Ungame with Carmen,
her husband and two children. Carmen was 43,
attractive and financially well off. *Here's a woman who*
has almost everything, I thought. Carmen drew a card
that asked her to talk about a hurtful moment.
"When I was six," she revealed to her family for the
first time, "my mother told me I was too old to be
kissed. I felt so bad that every morning I went into
the bathroom and looked for the tissue on which
she'd blotted her lipstick. I carried it with me all day.
Whenever I wanted a kiss, I rubbed the smear of
lipstick against my cheek."
Carmen's life had not been as perfect as I'd
thought. For almost forty years she had endured this
small, private heartache. *Can anyone make up for that?*
I wondered.
Several turns later, Carmen's eight-year-old son
landed on a comment space. Quietly, he got up and
walked over to his mother. Without a word, he put

his thin arms around her neck and kissed her on the cheek. Carmen's eyes filled with tears. The old hurt was gone—perhaps for good.[5]

What can you do to touch your special person with the accepting, unconditional love of God?

LISTENING

Dependent	Independent	Interdependent
Listens intently to get clues on how to "fit in."	Better talker than listener; listens when it serves his/her purposes.	Listens to better understand mate, self, and to get a broader perspective.
Listens for feelings and words.	Can ignore words and feelings behind them.	Listens for feelings as well as words.
Listens defensively.	Listens defensively.	Listens with feedback and acceptance.
Internalizes criticism.	Rejects criticism.	Weighs criticism.

9

Making Conflict a Double Win

FROM CONTROL TO COLLABORATION

*If a person feels ignored he/she may pick
a fight just to get some communication going!*

If our economic system failed at the rate that marriages do, we'd all be living in the forest, eating wild berries and the bark off trees. It's no secret that we are a throwaway society. What did you do with yesterday's empty milk carton, orange juice container, and the junk mail? We can easily be pressured by the media to get into the habit of thinking our spouses are disposable too—especially when they disagree with us.

And disagree they will! To some of us, conflict is highly uncomfortable. Others of us can't feel at home without some kind of swirling controversy because our childhood homes were troubled. Whether we're uncomfortable or at ease with conflict, it still is a part of any relationship. Can you come out of a conflict valuing yourself and your partner, motivated by love, or are you doomed to be controlling in your use of power?

When there is conflict, it doesn't mean there is something wrong with your mate, you, or your marriage.

Conflict is simply a point of view. If you have a great marriage, the two of you will not always agree. If you have a lousy one, you will be in total agreement at all times.

The more diverse your backgrounds, the more conflict will arise. Understand that, expect that, and embrace that. The first years of marriage are extraordinarily challenging. Half of all divorces happen in the first seven years. One of the big issues to settle in the early stages of marriage is how you, as a couple, handle conflict.

The best marriage will not protect us from the situations that make life challenging—struggle, illness, boredom, anger, disappointment, and mistakes. Conflict just means that it's time to go back to the drawing board, always with the bottom-line understanding that your marriage is a mutual, permanent, and exclusive union.

What you disagree about doesn't matter half as much as *how* you disagree. Conflict itself is not the problem. It demonstrates that you both care. Our reactions to conflict are what cause the problems.

Give Yourself Permission to Disagree

It is a fantasy to expect that two people, no matter how much they love each other, will grow at the same rate, in the same direction, and will face issues having the same perspective. That would be tremendously boring. There would be no stretching of the attitudes, yet that is the very perspective we often bring to marriage.

Be thankful and embrace conflict. We are commanded to give thanks in all things. God has something to teach us that we need to learn. If there is only one side to an issue, then only half of the truth is known.

The Goals of Conflict

One of the major goals in the midst of conflict needs to be the developing of an openness to discover a more complete sense of the truth. Another goal needs to be to change patterns of dealing with conflict that haven't been effective in the past. The new tools we have introduced to you in this book may feel unnatural now, but you may have been dissatisfied with what you've been doing naturally.

The last goal of conflict is to open up blocked lines of communication, while projecting the conviction that whatever is wrong is temporary. After all, you have faith in God, you respect yourself, you respect your mate, and you are in search of the best possible solution to the problem confronting you. Affirm that mutual understanding is what you both are after. One of you is not out to change the other. Acknowledge that when there is a problem, it is a "couple problem" about which you *both* need to communicate. What an exciting opportunity this is to understand both yourself and your mate better.

Give Yourself Permission to Change

When we try a recipe that doesn't work, we throw it out and never use it again. When we are ineffective in our communication patterns, we often repeat the same patterns over and over again at an accelerating pitch out of desperation.

What are our options during a time of conflict? We can choose to yield, withdraw, win, or struggle together through to resolve. There are extremely serious consequences if one of these patterns becomes habitual.

When we entered marriage, my pattern was to yield and Jan's was to win. This should not be too surprising given the home backgrounds we both experienced.

I had an extremely handicapped sister. She was unable to talk, walk, feed herself, or use her hands in any way.

Raised voices had a very negative effect on her, and she would start to cry. You can imagine the effect that had on my honest expression of frustration. It just wasn't allowed. The unspoken message in my house? "Good Christian families don't raise their voices. In fact, they don't have conflict."

Jan grew up in a home where a good discussion and argument was one of the ways to improve your complexion. Her family enjoyed examining many perspectives, but often each member held rather tightly to his/her own opinions. As a result, Jan grew up verbal and opinionated.

You can imagine what happened in our home. I consistently retreated and yielded and Jan became very proficient at going for the jugular. If she just lambasted me with words, I would yield and the issue would never have to be dealt with. Neither of us was being honest.

Do You Yield?

What is the result in your life if you are a consistent yielder? It is possible to yield before your partner is even aware that you disagree. I often did this early in our marriage, rather than muddy the waters. Jan didn't realize I had differing opinions because I held them inside. It doesn't take very long until yielders honestly believe that they don't count—only their mates do. In many ways yielders live under their mates, all the while telling themselves it doesn't really matter. Yielders deny past hurts and pretend that all is forgotten. They repress past resentments, feelings, and thoughts, and respond according to whatever their spouses expect. This is not forgiveness, it is fantasy. In reality yielders are extremely angry people, but they play the "good Christians don't get angry" tape in their minds. They are sticks of dynamite waiting to explode.

Often midlife is when the emotional TNT goes off. Perhaps you've heard the words: "You've had your way all these years. Now it's my turn. I'm going to do my own thing." Off he/she drives in a bright-red Porsche, leaving the spouse dumbfounded. After all, they *never* argued.

Do You Win?

Yielders are often married to persons who feel compelled to win. They believe that they count but the yielder and his/her opinions are expendable. These people live against and over their partners. They will often do or say anything it takes to win. They deliver hurt and are highly destructive in their use of anger.

Do You Withdraw?

Still others withdraw. Remember, the opposite of love is not hate; it is indifference. If you are married to a withdrawer, you know what indifference feels like. The withdrawer removes himself/herself from not only the conflict but also the relationship. The message given out is that neither person counts but neither does their relationship: "I live in spite of you and I live without you." How manipulative this method is! The withdrawer disconnects emotionally from hurt, while all the time delivering the hurt of indifference. The anger in this relationship is highly destructive because the withdrawer turns away from his/her spouse and the issue. Distance is created and any hope of resolution is dashed.

Can Resolution Happen?

Resolution happens when we understand our mate's point of view and allow it to affect our original opinion. We take the time to walk in our spouse's moccasins.

Resolution is the goal of the partnership marriage. It takes longer—yes! Resolvers mutually respect each other. Together they discuss the hurt. Their anger is constructive because it is honestly communicated. They affirm each other and together direct their anger toward whatever it is that is dividing them.

Regardless of the conflict, whether it be over finances, church, in-laws, children, sex, or whatever, the statement most often spoken by the yielder is, "I must have seen it wrong. You're right, of course." The withdrawer often says, "What problems? I don't want to discuss it." The winner often is overheard saying something like, "How could you be so stupid?" The resolver stands in front of his/her mate and says, "I value you. I'm hurt that something is dividing us. I disagree with you right now, but I want to understand your perspective, and I need you to listen to mine."

There are definitely times to yield. As mentioned earlier, perhaps the issue at hand doesn't matter a great deal to you but it matters a lot to your mate. Maybe you discover after communicating that you are wrong. Then yield because love means *often* having to say you're sorry.

There also are times to withdraw—but only if you agree to come back and discuss the issue at a mutually acceptable time. This is especially important if you have a temper. Perhaps you would be wise to discipline yourself to discuss the issue when you're calmer. If the argument begins at midnight, you might be wiser to insist on getting a good night's sleep and discussing the conflict in the morning.

Pause and think through the following questions. Your spouse's and your happiness may depend on it!

Which style of conflict do you usually use?
Which style does your mate use?
How do you feel about your style?
How do you feel about your mate's style?

Often we discover a lot of things that don't work in the process of discovering what does. Perhaps it is time to throw out the old recipe and try a new one.

CONFLICTING STYLES OF CONFLICT RESOLUTION[1]

Dependent	Independent	Interdependent
Takes orders without asking questions.	Gives orders without asking questions, without permitting questions.	Asks questions, seeks to truly hear, suggests alternatives.
Obeys demands.	Makes demands, dishes out directions, defensive if challenged.	Respects freedom and dignity of others, can affirm the truth clearly and concretely, but nondefensively.
Complies regardless of feelings.	Requires compliance regardless of consent or agreement.	Values willing cooperation, works for open agreement and understanding.

CONFLICTING STYLES OF
CONFLICT RESOLUTION[1]

Dependent	*Independent*	*Interdependent*
Stays in under position.	Pushes and manipulates one-man rule in over-under position.	Leads, attracts, persuades personal relationships in side-by-side identification.
Says, "I will." "I should." "I must."	Says, "You do." "You must do." "You ought to." "You'd better do."	Says, "Come, let's do." "We might have done." "Can we try?"
Depends on others to motivate.	Depends on his/her own external authority to motivate others.	Depends on internal integrity to motivate them.
Tries to keep peace at any cost.	Generates friction, resistance, and resentment.	Generates acceptance, cooperation, and reconciliation.
Pleases but frustrates people by indecision.	Separates and isolates people.	Unites and helps persons relate to one another.

Questions to Ask Yourself if You Need to Win

Through the use of power, you may have chosen or gotten into the habit of being aggressive. You have been bullying your mate to get him/her to agree with you. You have been disregarding your spouse's rights or feelings and thought only of your own.

Here is a group of questions you will want to ask yourself:

Do I feel I'm in competition with my spouse?
Why am I afraid of being vulnerable?
Why do I view vulnerability as a weakness?
Why am I afraid of listening to my spouse?
Do I really believe that my spouse is my equal?
What tools do I use to ensure that I win?
Do I believe that the Holy Spirit is in me and not in my mate?
Can I, over the long run, really love and respect someone I intimidate?
The benefits of needing to win are. . . .
The disadvantages are. . . .
What would happen to me if I gave up my position of power?

There is a very wise old adage: Do not make yourself so big; you're really not so small.

Suggestions for the Yielder

Others have made the choice to yield. Perhaps you need to examine why you are so uncomfortable with conflict. Is it possible that you don't know how to deal with an overbearing partner? Yielders usually have two things in common—they don't know how to say no, and they want everyone's approval. Let us introduce you to the "No Sandwich Technique."[2] It will literally change your relationship.

No Sandwich Technique

First Layer: A statement that acknowledges you heard what the other person wants you to do. Practice your feedback skills. Example: "I understand that you want me to drop everything and take the car in to be serviced."

Second Layer: Your refusal and why you will not or cannot comply with his/her wishes. Example: "But I am facing a deadline to get an important project of mine finished."

Third Layer: An affirmation of your mate or something you are able to do to ease the sting of your refusal. Example: "I will be finished with my work in two hours. I will be happy to take the car in then if it will help."

Here is the "No Sandwich Technique" used in another scenario:

"I understand you want me to watch a pornographic movie with you.

"But I choose not to fill my mind with entertainment that degrades women, men, and sex. I also believe that what goes into my mind can defile me. It's threatening to my femininity when you choose a counterfeit for the real thing.

"I'd love to spend an intimate evening together. You're more exciting to me than any movie would ever be."

It might also be extremely helpful for you to memorize these generic statements if you are very passive:

"I understand that you want me to. . . ."

"I am unable to do what you demand. If I did I would
not be true to myself."

"I am willing to talk to find something agreeable. I
value you and our relationship."

If your mate keeps persisting in his/her attempt to
control you, use what communication experts call the
"Broken Record Technique." You are to repeat your "No
Sandwich" statements as many times as needed with a
firm but calm and quiet voice. You can refuse to be
controlled by intimidation.

Practicing the "No Sandwich Technique" will move you
toward being assertive. You are being clear, direct, and
open about your feelings, thoughts, and desires. You are
cultivating self-awareness. (*What do I really think about this
and why?*) You are being respectful, not only of your
partner's rights but also of your own.

Questions to Ask a Mate Who Withdraws

If your mate's typical response is to leave the room
whenever you have a disagreement, you are definitely
feeling angry and frustrated. In many ways you probably
feel hopeless and unloved. Here are some questions we
suggest you ask your mate when you both calm down:

"I'm hurt/angry. Did you intend that?"

"What can I do to make it easier for you to stay and
face this issue with me?"

One of Dave's clients expressed her frustration beautifully
to her mate:

The thing I want most is to protect my love for you.
I never want to feel paralyzed. I never want to feel

dead inside. So, I need to tell you when I am hurting or angry. That's one of the ways I take care of our relationship.

Give Yourself a Temperature Check

Anger is a signal that "I don't like what is happening." It is a normal emotion that is trying to tell you something about yourself and your relationship.

Anger isn't harmful to relationships unless it is stashed away, denied, or expressed in such a way that we end up accelerating the emotions we feel. Often anger is just an external result of an internal cause—hurt, fear, frustration, dashed expectations, and a wounded self-esteem.

Each of us needs to control our tendency, when we are angry, to reach for words that will hurt our mates. Have you ever been involved in an argument and discovered that all your energy was spent on self-defense instead of on solving the problem? Insults and blows aren't necessary. They are the result of denying your anger too long.

One of the most important questions to ask ourselves in the midst of conflict is, *How have I contributed to the problem?* Do you insist on having the last word? Pride cometh before divorce. Certainly we are not responsible for everything that goes wrong in our marriages. We are not responsible for our mates' actions or reactions. What we are responsible for is our personal actions and attitudes. Our peace doesn't depend on anyone else's behavior—we have to answer to God alone for what kind of a marriage partner we have been.

We can't control how a marriage partner will treat us. We all have desires, but there is no guarantee that our spouses will meet them. When an expectation is not met, we hurt, and it is natural to want to lessen the pain. Insults, scorn, and temper tantrums never lessen the pain;

they create more intense pain. All we can do is to talk honestly about our disappointments with our spouses. If he/she ignores our words, we must take our hurts to the Lord. James 4:1 makes it very clear that the source of conflicts is within us. When there is a war going on inside us, there is a natural tendency to murder one another with our tongues. James warns us to keep our tongues under control so we can keep our bodies under control.

If you feel your temperature rising, it is wise to ask yourself these questions:

Am I angry at my mate for failing to live up to my expectations?
Am I angry at myself?
Am I afraid, frustrated, hurt, or is my self-esteem low?
What really made me angry?
Have I shared my anger honestly with my mate?

Has your spouse ever rejected your response to his/her hurt? It could be that you haven't listened long enough. It may help to say, "I can see you are really hurting. Is there more you want to tell me?" Some couples have found that writing letters to one another helps when they are intensely hurt or angry.

Be aware that no matter how wisely you express your anger, your mate may feel attacked and become defensive. This could be a reaction to childhood experiences involving excessive criticism. Somehow the expression of anger is associated with either a loss of love or with terrifying retaliation.

Often we enter marriage with the basic assumption that the two of us can handle anything. That may not be true. Perhaps our anger stems from the residue of a past relationship, our own immaturity, or physical or emotional abuse.[3] Whatever the cause, do not be afraid to search out professional assistance if your relationship seems to be characterized by extreme and constant anger.

Get to the Real Issue

Sometimes we repeatedly come against one issue when we're really angry about another. If your disagreement seems to go round and round, you're not touching the real issue; you're not hearing the heart talk. What is your spouse trying to tell you? Once that has been identified, it is easier to work through your disagreements.

If you are caught in the midst of an attack, perhaps the sharp words are covering up less easy-to-articulate feelings. Is your beloved afraid of being hurt; is he/she longing to be reassured of your love and commitment or needing to be closer? Do your choice of words and attitudes antagonize your spouse? Does your mate believe that you are open to listen to his/her perspective? Does he/she feel fairly treated? Is he/she threatened by a competitive spirit?

Help in clarifying the real issue. Role play each other's position. Feedback to see if your position is clearly articulated. Discuss each other's position.

In the midst of conflict, both of you are probably asking the same question: "How can I fully understand you and still be me?" We must, for this reason, polish up our listening skills. Wait until your mate has said what he/she really means before jumping in. Resist the urge to be a grasshopper. Always invite your mate to participate in the solution. People who want their marriages to work take the time to reach decisions that are mutually satisfying.

Search for areas of agreement. Affirm your love for each other often, and if you are able to resolve, establish a joint goal. Make the issue a double win whenever it is possible.

The challenge of conflict:
How can I
fully understand you
and
still be me?

When you've thoroughly hashed things through, give each other a reconciliatory hug—or two or three.

Give Yourselves Permission to Disagree

Sometimes you'll disappoint each other and sometimes you'll absolutely amaze each other with your sensitive understanding. There have been times in our relationship when we have both felt too strongly about an issue to be able to resolve it quickly. Those are the times we agree to disagree. For us that is a signal that we need to take the matter to the Lord in prayer separately. He is more than capable of showing either or both of us the weaknesses in our opinion. It is the time to learn as much as we can about this issue. It is also necessary to face some questions:

Can I communicate my opinion more effectively?
Does my mate know that I value him/her and his/her opinion even though we are disagreeing?
Could I be standing in the way of my spouse's growth by not resolving this issue?
Could I accept my partner's decision?

This is not the time to pull in a third party. This is not the time to clam up. If either of you choose silence, the decision will be made based on only half the truth. Both of you will be bound by the smallness of one partner's perspective. One or two statements a day left unsaid become in a short time three or four subjects. Over a period of time we become strangers to each other.

Let's have great marriages, in which the two of you agree to disagree so that any decisions you make can be based on at least two perspectives. It takes effort to move from controlling your partner to collaborating with him/her, but it's the difference between an unhappy marriage and a great one. It's also the difference between the love of power and the power of love.

TEN WAYS TO DEAL WITH CONFLICT IN A PARTNERSHIP MARRIAGE

1. Both partners need to agree that this is an appropriate time to work out this conflict.
2. Pick a neutral place to discuss the issue. (Sometimes the home is an emotionally charged arena.)
3. Identify the real issue that needs to be discussed.
4. Affirm that the two of you are united against the issue or wall that is dividing you. Attack the problem and not each other. The goal is a deeper understanding rather than winning or losing a battle.
5. Listen to your partner's words and feedback. Example: "What I hear you saying is. . . ."
6. Share your own position honestly and clearly, using *I* statements: "I feel. . . ." "I think. . . ." "I need. . . ." Avoid those attacking *You* statements: "You always . . ." or "You never. . . ."
7. Attempt to lower your voice one notch instead of raising it two.
8. Avoid the temptation to be historical and bring up past hurts. When you're wrong, admit it.
9. Resist the temptation to yield or withdraw (either emotionally or physically) before a solution is reached.
10. When you have come to a decision, do not raise it again. You're on the same team and have now made your decision.

A MEETING OF HEARTS

Check your own opinion in the appropriate column.

	Husband's Desires			Wife's Desires		
	wants less	*wants same*	*wants more*	*wants less*	*wants same*	*wants more*
1. I enjoy sharing hobbies, sports, and fun times with my spouse.						
2. I enjoy the relaxing times we share together.						
3. I enjoy the way we communicate about daily lives and events.						
4. I enjoy being with my spouse.						
5. I appreciate time to be by myself.						

	Husband's Desires			Wife's Desires		
	wants less	*wants same*	*wants more*	*wants less*	*wants same*	*wants more*
6. I openly express my own feelings to my spouse and tell him/her what I need and enjoy.						
7. I enjoy our conversations about our personal spiritual journey.						
8. I enjoy our marriage-centered rather than child-centered home.						
9. I enjoy our sexual relationship.						
10. I enjoy working toward shared goals.						

A MEETING OF HEARTS

Check your own opinion in the appropriate column.

	Husband's Desires			Wife's Desires		
	wants less	*wants same*	*wants more*	*wants less*	*wants same*	*wants more*
11. I enjoy the relationship we share with each other's parents.						
12. I enjoy the relationship we share with our children.						
13. I enjoy my spouse's friends.						
14. I enjoy the time we share with other couples.						
15. I appreciate the way my spouse encourages me to develop my hobbies, talents, qualities, and gifts.						

	Husband's Desires			Wife's Desires		
	wants less	*wants same*	*wants more*	*wants less*	*wants same*	*wants more*
16. I enjoy the feeling of being an important partner in this marriage.						
17. I enjoy the emotional support I receive from my partner.						
18. I enjoy working together on our financial commitments and goals.						
19. I enjoy the variety and spice in our married life.						

A MEETING OF HEARTS

Check your own opinion in the appropriate column.

	Husband's Desires			Wife's Desires		
	wants less	*wants same*	*wants more*	*wants less*	*wants same*	*wants more*
20. I appreciate that our home is a fun place for all of us to come home to.						
21. I appreciate the way we communicate about our differences.						
22. I am happy about the way we settle our differences.						
23. I appreciate the loyalty and affirmation I receive from my spouse.						

	Husband's Desires			Wife's Desires		
	wants less	*wants same*	*wants more*	*wants less*	*wants same*	*wants more*
24. I appreciate the effort my spouse takes to keep himself/herself physically attractive.						
25. I enjoy the safe feeling that comes when I know I am forgiven for past failures.						

10

Physical Intimacy: Satisfying, Sensual, and Spiritual

FROM INHIBITED TO INITIATOR

*Lord, help us find those places in us which
we have never opened to your love. Show us
the subterranean chambers we have forgotten,
the dark rooms where some small part
of us is hiding. These too we hope to share—
the musty and the moldy, the decayed and the
rancid. Cleanse us that we might more
fully uncover all of us, known and unknown.
Beginning now, lead us toward a total
relationship with each other
and with you.*

CHARLIE AND MARTHA SHEDD [1]

We played a word association game with each other
before writing this chapter. Our word was *sex*. Here
are our responses:

good	**healthy**
creative	**fascinating**
wonderful	**restful**
gift	**sexy**
positive	**uninhibited**
pure	**exhilarating**
exciting	**ageless**
celebration	**holy**

and fun

What words would you have chosen? We love loving each other but our feelings were not always so positive. The difference between sex being something that you do for your partner and the opinion we now hold—that it is something we both enjoy and need—came when we changed our attitudes. We share these "lessons" with you in hopes that your relationship will be transformed as radically by them as ours was.

Accept God's Word

God wants you to enjoy sex! It is a gift created by the same tender Savior who loved each of us enough to give us the ultimate gift of Himself. Love is God's absolute bottom line. In fact, God is love. The closer we get to this kind of a God—the more we learn to "let go"—the greater the possibility of drawing closer to our mates.

Our expression of love to each other can be a taste of the divine on earth if we agree with Scripture that sex is one of God's good and perfect gifts. After God created male and female, the words in Genesis 1:31 are:

And it was very good.

So God made man like his Maker: Like God did God make man; Man and maid did he make them. . . . Then God looked over all that he had made, and it was excellent in every way . . . (Genesis 1:27, 31 TLB).

". . . he was very pleased . . ." (Genesis 1:31 Good News Bible).

"And He approved it completely . . ." (Genesis 1:31 AMPLIFIED).

That's mighty different from the "I'll just do my duty but don't expect me to enjoy it" or the "Men are just animals" attitudes. We're so glad it's different.

In our marriages, let's allow the inner presence of the Holy Spirit to free us up to increasingly enjoy what God has approved of completely.

Accept Your Own Body

We cannot have satisfying sex if we are uncomfortable with each other's bodies, visually and tactilely. Our enjoyment will be decreased if we refuse to appreciate and accept our own bodies.

If you feel shame and self-consciousness when your partner's eyes look at you naked, it is enough to keep you from relaxing into your sexual feelings. Have you ever faced your uncomfortable feelings long enough to ask where they came from?

Three factors determine our body image. They are feedback, sensory input, and the models we hold to. What type of feedback have you gotten from childhood on about your body? The feedback could have come from peers, brothers or sisters, mother or dad, teachers, friends, or enemies. What nicknames were pinned on you? Many of us are prone to defining ourselves in the eighties in the same way that a negative voice did in our past.

The amount of touching that you received in your home also affects your body image. Did you learn that you were indeed touchable? Did you learn that if you touched yourself you would be cruelly and severely punished? If this was the case it probably didn't take you long to realize that parts of your body were "bad."

What models do you hold up as ideal? We live in a culture that says we have to earn our value by how we look. So we spend the vast majority of our time comparing ourselves to others. The purpose of the billion-dollar cosmetic industry is to persuade us all that we need help— some a little and some a lot. The result? We grow up with insecurities. How can it be any different if we settle for a Jane Fonda or Tom Selleck ideal? In this arena we compare our worst, of which we are most aware, with everyone else's best, which is all we ever see. What a negative impact this has on our sexual intimacy!

Do you care enough about God, yourself, and your spouse to move against a negative body image? It is possible to choose to feel differently, and we are delighted to share the steps we found personally helpful.

Get Into God's Word. We must not be ashamed to consider what God wasn't ashamed to create! What does God say about your body?

> Psalms 139:14 (KJV): "I will praise thee; for I am fearfully and wonderfully made."

> Proverbs 5:18, 19 (NAS):
> Let your fountain be blessed,
> And rejoice in the wife of your youth.
> As a loving hind and a graceful doe,
> Let her breasts satisfy you at all times;
> Be exhilarated always with her love.

When was the last time you read Song of Solomon out loud to each other? If the language is incomprehensible to you, we suggest a book to accompany your Scripture reading. It is *Solomon On Sex* by Joseph C. Dillow (Thomas Nelson Publishers), and we guarantee that the two of you will have a wonderful time.

The wonder, awe, and excitement with which God views our bodies needs to be contrasted with the negative feedback you received as a child and that you have been feeding on today. As an adult you must make a choice: which voice are you going to meditate on? It's your decision.

Get Comfortable With Your Own Body. Most people who don't like their bodies rarely, if ever, look at them. Self-image often exists only in the imagination. Rare is the woman who is pleased with how her breasts look. The real problem is that they don't look the way they did on Barbie dolls, starlets, or "siliconized" Playmates. You may be a Christian but you do live in this world, and its standards for beauty affect you. We can complain about our bodies so long that we finally convince ourselves and our mates that we are unattractive. Be wise.

If you are grateful for the body God gave you and if you are willing to look at its beauty, you will become attractive to yourself and then to your mate. When you do this the first few times, you will no doubt be embarrassed. We hope that you have a full-length mirror in your bedroom. It isn't enough to just have one, however. It must be used!

LOVE THYSELF EXERCISE

For five private minutes each day, get undressed and look yourself over—head to toe—in front of a full-length mirror. Focus on what you find attractive. . . . If we're honest, all of us have lines and parts and special angles of our bodies which we like, just as when we look at our faces in the mirror we have favorite "views" and "poses" which please us. Don't look at your "figure"; look at pleasing lines and forms. For once, focus on what you like about your body instead of what you do not like.

All the while, talk to yourself, giving a running commentary on what you see; for example: "There is something soft and inviting about my neck, isn't there. No wonder he likes to snuggle there. . . ." Or, for a man: "When I stand straight, my shoulders do have a strong, square look. Not bad." Don't miss a spot. Give yourself a real once-over.[2]

God created that body. It is wonderously made. It pleased Him.

Do you know what your genitals look like? Take the time to examine them in the mirror, too. Perhaps to your surprise, you will discover that they don't look "grotesque" or "dirty." God approved of them. Get familiar with how they really look. Sex begins with a relaxed appreciation of your own body.

Get Some Feedback From Your Spouse. We attended one of Cliff and Joyce Penner's weekend retreats. It was outstanding. Together they have written *The Gift of Sex: A Christian Guide to Sexual Fulfillment* (published by Word Books). We recommend this.

At the seminar, we were given a homework assignment. It was one of the most difficult and freeing things for us personally. We recommend it highly.

Stand in front of a full-length mirror stark naked. Your partner is to sit on the bed and be completely still. You are to talk about your feelings about every part of your body, including the genitals. Start at the top of your head and work down to your toes.

What do you like?

What don't you like?

When you are finished talking, your husband/wife is to tell you how he/she feels about your body.

Listen and accept.

Together, thank God for the wonder of His creation.

How healing it is when we let ourselves hear words carrying this sentiment:

Many men would agree mountains are beautiful and sunsets, oceans, rivers, brooks, lakes, each have their particular glory. Ditto for the night sky, the stars, full moon. For the day sky, too, sunrise, white clouds, the birds in flight, rainbow, and the majesty of a storm.

Yet still, with all these splendors, some of us would say, "I am married to the most beautiful sight in the world. Thank you, Lord."[3]

Exercise. You just knew we'd say it, didn't you! Staying in shape physically is the main way we can stay in shape sexually. It is possible that you really are too tired for sex. Rest isn't the answer; exercise is.

We can't guarantee that you will live longer but you will live with more enthusiasm and you'll love better. Sex is a physical act. The most satisfying sex begins when we are completely relaxed. There is no more effective way to become relaxed and ready for love than physical exercise. Could you and your mate take a brisk walk each evening? Try to get your walking up to thirty minutes.

Get Lots of Sensory Experiences. Do you feel that every

time your spouse touches you it will lead to intercourse? If so, this habit pattern must be broken. Touch is healing. There needs to be much touching of each other without demand. Do you snuggle up to your love when he/she is reading or watching TV? Let him/her know that touching is pleasure enough.

Pray Together and Separately. Praise and thank God for the marvelous gift He has given both of you. After you have enjoyed making love, don't turn over in bed like you're a big bump on a log or a hibernating bear. Hold each other tight and praise God for each other and the gift of sex. Perhaps then you can enjoy a bubble bath and touch and talk and pray and touch some more.

Affirm Each Other Over and Over and Over Again.

> "You've got the greatest body."
> "I desire your touch."
> "You are so beautiful/handsome."

Accept That It Doesn't Come Naturally

When talking to a group of husbands, Ed Wheat said, "If you do what comes naturally in lovemaking, you can almost count on being one hundred percent wrong." Men are aroused by what they see, while most women need tender words and touch. Solomon grasped this truth. He admired every part of his new bride's body and told her so. A woman needs tender, explicit words. Both sexes yearn to be touched. In fact, the Lord created a woman's clitoris to give her sexual pleasure. It has no other purpose. We all crave touching and affection for its own sake—not just as a means to a sexual end.

Wives and husbands must communicate clearly to one another what gives them pleasure. We recommend much nondemand pleasuring when both of you are naked. You take your mate's hand, tell him/her what feels good, and show him/her how to touch you. Then listen as he/she does the same to you. Caress each other's bodies and talk about the sensations. Always move toward positive feelings. Every relationship needs gentle, unhurried, nondemanding love play. If you don't take the time to learn what makes your partner tick, you're going to learn what makes him/her ticked.

There Are Myths in Need of Rejection

If you have a good relationship—including servanthood, mutual respect, and communication—your sex life will take care of itself. This is false! We have to learn how to be a skillful giver and a responsive, enjoying receiver. After denying ourselves for all the years that we were single, it is unrealistic to expect to be instantly turned on after the wedding ceremony. Some have past memories to move against. Drop this unrealistic expectation.

A little boy was asked how he learned to skate. His reply was, "By getting up every time I fall down." This is also true in the sexual arena. You're not weird if you have struggles in your sex life; you're normal. With every change there will be frustrations. Just as it takes years for babies to grow, give your marriage time.

The perfect mood will strike, and I will be ready for love. Magic is not in charge of your sex life—you are! People who wait for the perfect inspiration rarely, if ever, have sex. Romantic ways to add sparkle to your marriage are viewed with a jaundiced eye. This person thwarts his/her own needs as well as his/her mate's.

Making love is an act that must be performed. If you swallow this lie, sex becomes a test with a potential for failure. We become little Boy Scouts working on merit badges. Sex is one of the greatest pleasures in life—if we understand that we are needing not to learn how to perform but to relax and enjoy sexual pleasure. Orgasm is not an end in itself.

If we perform, we focus on our mate's responses and we forget about our own feelings. At that point our lovemaking becomes pressured, polite, and mechanical. It leads to a preoccupation with how you look and sound rather than enjoying your feelings. Orgasm at its best is a total loss of control. To your mate, the sights and sounds of total abandonment are a wonder. The rest is playacting.

Playful and exciting sex is not for mature married people. How sad! Once we take our marriage vows, sex becomes a "should." It can become a routine that causes couples to drift into sexual apathy. Making love in the same way every time can be compared to eating the same menu each day for the rest of your life. What a drudgery. Many couples use marriage to turn themselves off and then they blame marriage. We turn ourselves on or off.

Sexual intercourse is the one and only type of sex for married couples. If you've swallowed this myth, you've got some fun research to do. Once again, we recommend Cliff and Joyce Penner's book *The Gift of Sex.*

Most women can have only one orgasm at a time. There are two extremes to be avoided. The first is a husband's insistence that his wife have multiple orgasms if one is all she prefers. The second is a fear that a woman desiring more means she is oversexed. In both cases women will often fail to communicate with their husbands, and this is destructive to a relationship.

The only good orgasm a woman can experience is one that is simultaneous with her husband. Attempts to climax at the same second can be self-defeating. Most men like to stop moving at the moment of orgasm. Most women like to keep moving. As we just noted, many women enjoy multiple orgasms, which they couldn't have if efforts at simultaneous orgasm failed. If this happens repeatedly, it can be highly frustrating. This myth forces us to be conscious of performing, and we tense up.

Every orgasm is inevitably an ecstatic experience. This is quite false. Some are deep and some are shallow and everything in between. It is foolish and self-defeating to expect this. With sex, getting there is more than half the fun.

The larger the penis, the greater the wife's satisfaction. The first one inch into the vagina has nerve endings that create pleasurable sensations. Past one inch the nerve endings are extraordinarily sparse. We believe that most men can manage one inch.

Contraception can create inhibition in our sexual relating. This will happen only if you let it, so why not make it a part of your love play. Your diaphragm could be inserted in front of your husband. It is not a turn-off. Both of you could put it in together. Don't hurry. Slip it in and out. Play doctor. Put the condom on together. Enjoy the sensations.

Within the Context of Marriage We Are Free to Experiment

There are two kinds of people in this world: those interested in sex and liars. Freedom enhances the sexual experience. The fewer so called rights and wrongs a couple has to limit their sexual relating with each other, the more spontaneity, flexibility, and experimentation the couple will enjoy.

The Bible gives no rules on *how* to make love but very clear guidelines about with whom one can make love. We agree with the Penners that the more conservative person should decide the guidelines within the marital relationship. It violates our mates to push them into any act. We call it marital rape. If one partner feels violated, the act is unnatural. We hope that the more conservative partner is open to change. A woman with noteworthy comments once wrote to Charlie and Martha Shedd:

> When I came down off my high and mighty and decided to be a missionary to my husband's needs psychologically, it was amazing the difference it made in our marriage, and I've gotten to the point where I enjoy every kind of sex with him now.[4]

Your Are the Best Authority on What You Need and Like Sexually

If you don't believe that you are the best authority, you may find excuses for not being involved sexually. In the absence of feedback, both men and women will often assume for years that what feels good to them also appeals to their spouses.

We need to be moving toward positive feelings. If our mates are unaware of what feels good to us, they cannot be expected to meet those needs. When a couple makes and believes the agreement that each will be responsible to let the other know what feels good and what does not, they have a great release of tension.

We please each other best by being honest with each other about our needs and our responses. We must change our focus from pleasing our partner or performing for our mates, to verbalizing our own pleasure to our mates. It is the most satisfying way to please our spouses.

Mutual Submission: You're Both Responsible for Initiating Physical Intimacy

Initiating sex is a conscious decision, not a sudden inspiration. The truth is, when we initiate we aren't feeling sexy, we are planning on it.

**Being selfish sexually
is the
best way
to serve your mate.**

Because it is a conscious decision, we are really saying that we want sex. That admission, rather than bringing joy, has the potential to bring anxiety and external guilt to some. Perhaps your childhood instruction taught that sex is dirty and bad, and you will be punished for enjoying it. If this is the case you may want to avoid sexual encounters.

There are so many diversions in our culture. We can overschedule; we can get involved in a TV program; we can be concerned about the children; we can be tired or sick; it can be too early or too late—or we may need more sleep.

> Even in the most "liberated" marriages where women do have careers, where household duties and child care are shared equally, back in the bedroom, they rarely have "initiation" rights. If the husband wants sex, he reaches for his wife's body; if she wants sex, she reaches for the perfume. And . . . it is not fair.[5]

If your husband has always initiated, he has never had the opportunity of experiencing sex as a demand, and you have never ever had sex because you wanted it.

In a power-hungry marriage, the husband uses sex to control his wife and she, in turn, refuses sex at all, showing him who is *really* in control. You need to relinquish the power and each initiate. This will give both of you the feeling of being wanted. We recommend that you alternate the initiation just as you alternate your date nights.

To begin with, there needs to be much nondemanding touching. Encourage the more hesitant partner to initiate. Sexual arousal is a pleasure in itself. We would recommend that you continue to make it a nondemand experience until your bodies have made friends.

Sometimes one of you will not be in the mood for sex. Every sexual refusal does not have to be viewed as a rejection. Many people don't initiate sex anymore because they can't risk a rejection. Establish between the two of you that there is freedom to refuse and that it is not rejection.

Your Husband/Wife Is Your Dream Lover

We recently received a memorable letter in the mail and we share a portion with you:

> Last week I had the pleasure and privilege of being visited by my friend of 20 years whom I hadn't seen in 10. I have been making myself crazy thinking about him.

The letter went on informing us of many of her hubby's failings and all of her past boyfriend's strengths. A rather unfair comparison, don't you think? There is no way that this woman can improve her relationship with her husband while fantasizing about loving someone else. It is our belief that if people would put half as much effort into making their sex life with their mates as exciting as they do into their extramarital affairs, their lives would be a lot happier.

> I have seen too many people who find the time to schedule clandestine assignations with their lovers, but who have never thought of scheduling an afternoon or evening of sex with their own wives or husbands; people who carefully search out romantic settings for their extramarital encounters but who never consider taking their marital sex lives out of their bedrooms at home and into a new and stimu-

lating setting; people who find the energy to make love all night with their lovers but who complain they are always too tired for sex at home; people who can get themselves in the mood for sex at a moment's notice with a lover, but who wait for the "perfect mood" to strike to make love at home; people who try all kinds of "crazy things" in bed with a secret lover, but who claim they feel shy or self-conscious about doing anything other than the "Real Thing" in their own bedroom. In short, people make extramarital sex fun, but insist that sex at home must be serious business.[6]

Let's have the best of both worlds as Christian couples. Let's have the security, love, and trust of a committed partnership and the thrill and adventure of an affair with our mates. Now we're ready for the fun. We share our ideas with you and encourage you to please write us and share yours with us.

A woman at one of our seminars was ready and waiting for her husband when he returned from work one day. She left a note on their front door—he was to follow the string. He opened the door to find a string on the doorknob leading to the bathroom. There was a bubble bath waiting for him, complete with candles. His wife had left a change of clothes there for him. After the bath he found ice and chilled cider in another sink. Then it led to his wife's closet, where he was to choose what he would like her to wear. Next it led to a candlelight dinner and finally into their bedroom. Dave calls this a progressive dinner!

One couple we know recently had a baby. The new mother was a little apprehensive about sex. She had just had a demonstration of the results! She was tired and amazed how little time she had for herself. The couple made a game of saying, "Do you want to make babies tonight?"

"Oh, no!"

"Terrific!" the other mate would reply. "Let's just have fun."

Schedule an evening of love play once a week. This is when you might buy a fast-food meal and some fresh cider on the way home from work. Take the food and each other to bed. No TV. Turn on the answering machine. You are going to have a nude picnic. Turn up the thermostat. Make it about four hours long. There is to be no end goal of orgasm. Whatever could you do for four hours? Mmmmm . . . .

- Eat, drink
- Talk, look
- Feel, touch with nondemand pleasuring
- Back rubs, tell jokes
- Use feathers, fur
- Read out loud, listen to music
- Giggle, finger paint each other's bodies
- Take a nap
- Do anything the two of you enjoy!

Make certain you have a lock on your bedroom door. Don't have the family TV in your bedroom. Older kids can honor your privacy. Tell them not to disturb you unless there is an emergency. They may giggle. That's great. You're modeling beautiful, healthy sexuality for them.

Instead of dining out, why don't you honeymoon out once a month? Hire a sitter. Then the two of you book into a hotel, without luggage, under a fantasy name or your real names.

Talk explicitly to your mate at surprise times. Get very good at whispering "sexy somethings" in his/her ear.

Take turns seducing one another.

Surprise one another. A couple at one of our seminars shared this fun idea. She had been away and she returned to find a poster welcoming her. The message on it had been written in a circular pattern so that it had to be turned to be read. She found out there was a present for her in bed. It was her husband, wearing a strategically placed bow.

Make love with lots of kissing, petting, and caressing with your clothes on.

A wife we know always had cold shoulders so she would wear something on top of her negligee. Her hubby told her he had solved both of their problems. He asked if she would wear one of his T-shirts to bed. She put it on only to find out that he had cut it under the arms—only her shoulders were covered!

Reenact absolutely fabulous memories you have had of satisfying sexual encounters with each other.

Pretend you are a geisha girl (if you're a she!).

Sleep in the nude once in a while.

Create an "I'm thinking of loving you" basket. What would you put in yours? Here are some suggestions:

- Scented bubble bath
- Candles

- Oil or lotion for a massage
- A tape of music that you find erotic
- Cider punch and two goblets
- Freshly ground coffee with two cups
- Your favorite men's/women's cologne
- Sexy underwear for both of you
- Finger paints; feathers
- A love letter from you
- Fresh flowers
- A tape telling your mate all the things you love about him/her and his/her body
- A book of poetry or a good book
- Fragrance

Play "doctor" or "I'll show you mine if you show me yours."

Kidnap your spouse or plan a mystery date.

This list is incomplete. That's your assignment. Find new ways to turn each other on for the rest of your lives. Sex is a beautiful gift from God. Celebrate it!

PHYSICAL INTIMACY

Dependent	*Independent*	*Interdependent*
I refuse, to show who is really in control.	I initiate, so that I am in control.	I initiate and respond to show my love.
I am a responder because this is my duty.	I initiate because this is my need.	I initiate and respond because this is our need.
I respond because my partner desires sex.	I initiate because I desire sex.	I initiate and respond because I desire sex.
I perform for my partner.	I please myself.	I please myself and respond better to my mate.

11

The Divine Wavelength

FROM PERFORMANCE TO PEACE

We were separate,
private and insular
until love
merged us,
enlarged us,
urged us to serve in union.
Now our goals peak higher than
our reach,
it seems,
sending us to our
book of directions for
getting there.
Taking in, filling up, we gather
strength to keep on giving out,
giving in, giving.

EILEEN JOHNSON[1]

Excerpted from "When Two Equal One" (Copyright © 1985 PARTNERSHIP Magazine). Used with permission.

The single most important aspect of our marriage together is our personal relationship with Jesus Christ. Our adequacy is not in ourselves but in God. Because of the Holy Spirit's influence in his life, Paul could say, "I can do all things through Him who gives me strength" (*see* Philippians 4:13). Because the Holy Spirit is active in our lives, we can affirm that mutual submission is possible. If we rely on our own strength, it is absolutely impossible. The command to mutual submission, found in Ephesians 5:21, is preceded by the command in verse 18 to be filled with the Spirit. Without the Holy Spirit active in our lives we are powerless and impotent in our loving.

The Holy Spirit desires to live His power through us. Each of us is called by Christ Himself to be Christ's feet, arms, hands, legs, smile, ears, and eyes to those special people we married. We are called to be God's love connection, but that is only possible if God is making His character traits a reality in our individual lives. Our emphasis doesn't need to be on whether we married the "right" partner; it needs to be whether, by the Holy Spirit's power, we are *becoming* the right partner.

Spiritual growth is the natural consequence of communion with God: "But the fruit of the Spirit is love, joy, peace, patience, kindness, goodness, faithfulness, gentleness, self-control . . . (Galatians 5:22, 23 NAS). This doesn't happen instantly, for we are in process. As you let God have more of you, He is ready to give you more of Himself. Your mate can't help but benefit.

Charlie and Martha Shedd ask these piercing questions:

"The fruit of the Spirit is *love.*" *Is there an increasing concern for each other in our marriage?*

"The fruit of the Spirit is *joy.*" *Are there increasing seasons of gladness in our relationship?*

"The fruit of the Spirit is *peace.*" *Is there an increasing quiet in our hearts, in our home, and in our lives?*

"The fruit of the Spirit is *longsuffering.*" *Is there an increasing stretch in our attitudes?*

"The fruit of the Spirit is *gentleness.*" *Are we increasingly kind, more courteous, softer in our touch?*

"The fruit of the Spirit is *meekness.*" *Is there a growing self-honesty in each of us?*

"The fruit of the Spirit is *goodness.*" *More and more do we seek to be a blessing?*

"The fruit of the Spirit is *faith.*" *These fears of ours, are they on a decline?*

"The fruit of the Spirit is *temperance.*" *Are we more and more in charge of our emotions?*[2]

In the spiritual area of your life, the condition of your heart becomes evident through your actions. But your goal is not right actions—it's communion with God. It's fascinating that the quality of life follows naturally. Being filled with the Spirit is not a performance; it is a way of life and a way of continually becoming.

In an interdependent partnership, there not only needs to be a genuine commitment to Christ, there also needs to be a hunger and a thirst for God on an ongoing basis. Each of us will benefit from following these guidelines for spiritual growth set out by J. Allan Petersen in his book *Before You Marry*:

1. Putting priority on daily time alone with God.
2. Talking freely to others about Christ.
3. Being sensitive to sin in your life and dealing with it.
4. Increasing in obedience to the Word of God.[3]

Only as we are personally growing in our communion with Jesus Christ and drinking deeply and consistently of His love and acceptance can we give to the person we live with. To give a gift freely, one must feel given to. Once again, we must affirm that this is only possible if Christ, not your husband, wife, or self, has first place in your life. We can't give what we haven't received. Without Christ's influence in our lives we don't know how to love, really love. We only know how to act out of duty, how to fake it, and how to take it.

Only as we love Jesus more than we love each other do we have the love we need to love each other with. We then become channels of God's love. There is something far more important in our marital relationships than pleasing each other or making each other happy. We are to put Christ first in both of our individual lives, so together we will love the Lord and become His channel to those in our lives.

Suggestions for Those Who Are Unequally Yoked

When either partner takes a step toward Christ-centered interdependence, the delicate balance in their relationship changes. Change can be frightening for both of you. Change almost guarantees that the person closest to you will try his/her hardest to push you back into your old ways of life. Every relationship seems to have an equilibrium, and when one mate initiates a change, the other often struggles to maintain the status quo.

If you are married to a non-Christian, you have a tremendous influence. Allow the Holy Spirit to make you into the most loving mate. First Peter 3:1, 2 tells us that your silent contribution to your marriage will be the best way of convincing your spouse to become a believer.

There are no guarantees that he/she will accept the Lord, however. For your own sake, as well as for the sake of your marriage, you need to maintain your commitment to be in communion with God, to obey Him, and then to minister to your spouse at every opportunity. Even if your spouse remains antagonistic to the Lord, you will experience a new level of spiritual growth and maturity.

Ways to Help Your Mate. This is a difficult situation for both of you. Regardless of whether you like them or not, accept your mate's feelings.

People don't change by being put down or evaluated. People change by being accepted. . . . Judgment does not change people. Take off the black robe and get out of the role of a judge. Deal with what is rather than what ought to be. Work toward acceptance rather than approval. Be *beside* the other person rather than on top of him. Acceptance is a suspension of judgment.[4]

Reassure your mate that your relationship is still top priority. To make this commitment come alive, let your mate determine how your time together is spent. That will give your mate a feeling of security in the midst of change. Encourage your wife/husband to do something new that perhaps has always been a special dream of theirs. Take particular care of your sex life. It will be a powerful way to demonstrate your unconditional love for your spouse.

Head-talk and heart-talk times are extremely crucial now. The best way to help your mate understand your love is to verbalize it to him/her. Keep quiet about your faith, unless asked; yet live out the fruit of the Spirit before his/her eyes. If asked, be ready to lovingly share your faith. Pray for your special person and for yourself.

What Can I Do for Myself? You need a Christ-centered, positive support group. The majestic redwoods, found in northern California, have a very shallow root system. It doesn't take much of a storm to topple one—unless they are growing in groves. In the midst of ferocious storms they stand tall because their root systems have intertwined. As our lives intertwine with positive, Christ-centered people, we stand tall in the midst of difficult times.

We received a letter from the most beautiful, courageous woman who finds herself unequally yoked. In the letter she shares that her first positive step had been to quit focusing on her husband and his faults and to begin facing areas where she needed personal growth. Then she flooded her mind with Scripture, using a planned memory system. Prayer and daily quiet times are a part of her spiritual disciplines. Then she shared with us that she is in a support group with other women who have non-Christian or unsupportive husbands. Together these incredible women have created some guidelines for their support group. We think they're fantastic.

1. *Focus on the good.*
   Dwell on things of good report. (*See* Philippians 4:8.) Cling to what is good. (*See* Romans 12:9.)
2. *Resist the temptation to talk about your spouse.*
   Reverence your husband. (*See* Ephesians 5:33.)
3. *Be more focused on what you can do rather than what your spouse is doing or not doing.*
   Each of us will give an account of himself before God. (*See* Romans 14:12.)
4. *Each day, try to commit to do some definite action for your spouse. Nail down exactly what you are going to do. How? When? Then report back to your support group when it is done.* (*See* Mattthew 7:24–27 and James 1:22–25.)
5. *Keep as your guide 1 Corinthians 13:4, 5* (TLB): "Love is very patient and kind, never jealous or envious, never boastful or proud, never haughty or selfish or rude. Love does not demand its own way. It is not irritable or touchy. It does not hold grudges and will hardly even notice when others do it wrong."
6. *No person will ever be able to meet the deep longing of your heart. Only God can do that.*
   (*See* 1 Thessalonians 2:4, 6; Colossians 3:23; 1 Corinthians 15:58; Hebrews 6:10.)

The words of this unequally yoked woman speak for themselves: "I can't begin to tell you the transformation in my life. Circumstances haven't changed (yet!) but God has changed my heart toward the circumstances." We ask you, can you do without such a support group if your mate doesn't share your enthusiasm for the Lord?

Suggestions to Those Who Are Unequally Yoked to Believers

Ideally, marriage is a covenant to mutual growth. However, what do you do if you have a hunger and thirst for God but your mate is not as willing to commit himself/herself to the discipline needed? What if you feel as if you're married to a spiritual giant, and you are but a baby? Hebrews 5:12–14 and 1 John 2:12–14 talk of levels of spiritual progress involving the infant, the youth, and the parent.

Sharon Drury wrote a thought-provoking article to women struggling with spiritual imbalances in their marriages in *Partnership* magazine. We paraphrase her wisdom with the prayer that your marriage will be strengthened by it.[5]

If you are spiritually more advanced than your mate, have patience. We all go through seasons. We're in process. None of us are finished products, thank the Lord. Don't judge your mate by your standards. Remember, acceptance is the only thing that leaves our spouses free to grow. Critique your own life rather than your mate's. Honestly affirm and esteem your mate for his/her good points. Perhaps you are not personally challenged enough. Maybe there is a place for your talent in the game rather than using all your energy to boo from the grandstand. Confess your prideful attitude to God and ask the forgiveness of your mate.

Perhaps you feel like a spiritual ant by comparison to your spouse. We want you to know that you can change some ineffective habits. This is not competition with your husband/wife; it is a communion with your God. Is Christ central in your life? If He is, your husband won't be. Take your hubby off the pedestal, and put God on. Remember the theme—progress, not perfection. God is your help so avoid knocking yourself down based on some unspoken "should." Get involved in disciplining someone who is a new Christian. He/she will keep you on your toes and accountable to steadily grow at your own pace.

Suggestions for Those Who Are Equally Yoked

You and your mate are "heirs together" of the grace of God. The Scriptures point out the interconnectedness of our marital and spiritual lives. First Peter 3:7 states that if a husband does not live in a considerate way with his wife, giving her respect as a fellow Christian, his prayers may be hindered. How we relate to each other affects our relationship with God. How we relate to God affects our marriages.

It seems as if we don't have to try terribly hard to come up with excuses for not growing together spiritually. We have three major forces pressuring us not to grow: the world, the flesh, and the devil. It seems to be easiest for us to succumb to the world's pressure by overscheduling our calendars. There is barely time to sleep, let alone to study. Our flesh fights us with attitudes of laziness, pessimism, and shallowness. Then there is Satan's pressure. In James 4:7, 8 we are told to resist the devil if we are going to draw near to God. Be aware of your enemies and control them, rather than letting them control you.

In the beginning God's Word called marriage into being. Now the Scriptures are crucial to our marriages. When a man and woman mutually agree to make Christ and His Words central in their individual lives and also in their

*Our emphasis doesn't need to
be on whether we married
the "right" person.
It needs to be,
by the Holy Spirit's power,
whether we are becoming
the "right" person.*

marriage, they begin to experience a marital transformation. The Scriptures become a daily guide to help develop the life pattern that will work for them. Their goal becomes a style of living that reflects Christ and thus produces satisfaction for both.

In good times Scripture enriches our individual and shared lives. In difficult times it undergirds and supports as it challenges us. In times of conflict it reminds us that the issue must be resolved or it will undermine our relationship. In betrayal times it rebukes us and challenges us to begin again. Are you and your spouse in the Scriptures together?

After a great deal of struggle in this area—and more than our share of failures—we have found something that works for us. Separately we read the same passage of Scripture on a daily basis. We both approach the passage with two questions: *What does it show me about God? What do You want from me, Lord?* Before we go to sleep at night we report our insights to one another. We share if there are things we don't understand and if there are matters we need to confess. Then we pray together. This works for us because separately we both are hungry for all of God, and yet we need to be held accountable to stick to the discipline of a quiet time. Some couples seem to be able to share their devotional time on a daily basis. That didn't work well for us. Our study habits are different, and our schedules are often in conflict.

We have also discovered that if we don't schedule our personal devotional times on a calendar, they never happen. In Hebrews 4:11 we are commanded to make every effort to enter into the rest. It takes discipline, it takes effort, and it takes scheduling.

Here are a few ways we enjoy growing together. We welcome your input if you have discovered other ways.

1. Charlie and Martha Shedd have what they call a mutual "self-analysis" time. They read the same section of a book or the Bible separately. As they are reading, they put marks in the margins:

Candle: A new thought. . . .
Arrow: "That hit me."
Question mark: "I don't quite understand this." . . .[6]

Then they get together at an agreed-upon time and discuss it. This can add some interesting conversation to your date night.

2. Pray together. Resist the temptation to protect yourself from each other. Rather, lift one another up to the Lord at all times. When we pray for each other and show concern for each other's spiritual growth, we are demonstrating powerfully that we love. God is a master heart changer. The tool He often uses is our prayer life. Evelyn Christenson was quoted as saying:

> Prayer, I believe, is the cement that holds a marriage together. You can't remain enemies and pray together. Those hurts and misunderstandings that come into all marriages melt away in the presence of a holy God. When you stand before God, there is no room for petty differences. There is no room for pride, or anger, or resentful feelings. Rather, there is power in your marriage and in your lives as the two of you agree together in prayer.
>
> Praying with my husband is a humbling experience. We often kneel and hold hands. When we invite the Holy God into our marriage, into our home, into our bedroom where we pray, it is bound to draw us together—and it has.[7]

3. Are you uncomfortable praying? Share your prayer requests verbally with each other and then pray silently, holding hands.

4. Dave sometimes shares his prayer requests, and then I pray for him. Then we switch. This is most effective when the issue to be prayed about is hurtful.

5. Read prayers out loud to God.

6. Pray through the Psalms. Paraphrase King David's praises.

7. Meditate in the same room over the same passage of Scripture. Try to picture it, hear it, smell it, and feel it. Then share your separate experiences with each other. "Be still and know that I am God" (*see* Psalms 46:10).

8. Read a devotional book using the tools of mutual self-analysis.

9. Sing hymns and praise choruses together. Play an instrument. Dave plays the violin and I the piano—for our own amazement and each other's amusement. Our praise time is enriched by this.

10. Disciple a small group separately. Come together and share the wonder of what the Lord is doing and what you're learning.

11. Write out your prayers and God's answers. Share a few.

12. Keep a journal.

13. Schedule an occasional weekend away to be together before the Lord. Work through your goals for your marriage, your children, and yourselves. Talk about how you can help each other achieve the desired goals.

14. Pray together for a couple who doesn't yet know the Lord or who is going through a separation

or divorce. Support them and love them through your actions.

15. Discuss the implications of Sunday's sermon in your life.

16. Set up a prayer calendar so you make it through all the prayer requests every week.

17. Take advantage of informal opportunities to share Jesus with each other; times when you are both in the car, going for a walk, doing errands, hiking, and so forth. God is closer to you than even your problems.

18. Take advantage of seminars, lectures, and outstanding movies and books.

19. Collect Christian music that ministers to the two of you.

20. Meditate on Psalms 34:1: ". . . his praise will always be on my lips." Cultivate an attitude of praise, positivity, and enthusiasm.

21. When your feelings are hurt, pray about it and ask yourself how your mate is hurting. Thank God that He has forgiven you for (*list specifics*) and affirm that *God* meets your needs. Be honest with your mate.

22. Be willing to admit it when you are wrong.

23. Once a week meet together and pray over each other's calendars. Ask yourselves what kind of a husband or wife you've been during the past week. Ask His help for the coming week. Our favorite time to do this is Sunday evening after the children have been tucked into bed.

Truly, love merges us, enlarges us, and urges us to serve. All these suggestions are not to put you under condemnation. They are not suggested to add yet another pressure, another "should." They are ways that together and separately you can commune with God. As we are in communion with Him, the Holy Spirit will create each of us into the right person for each other. The Holy Spirit will also set us free.

In her book *Finding Inner Security*, Jan shares the specifics of how we are set free in Christ. We share a portion of these with you. In an interdependent partnership we are free because the Holy Spirit has set us free:

 . . . .Free to define who I am but not to define who you are;

 . . . .Free to reach out to others but not to make yourself responsible for their choices;

 . . . .Free to love but not to lean. . . .

 . . . .Free to be married but never to forget you are a person. . . .

 . . . .Free to lead but not free to lord it over others;

 . . . .Free to affirm but not to manipulate, pretend, or blame. . . .

 . . . .Free to submit but not to be a doormat;

 . . . .Free to define your own needs and dreams and see them become a reality but not at the expense of those you care for. . . .

 . . . .Free to realize your equality but not to use it as an excuse for refusing to serve;

 . . . .Free to talk but not at the expense of listening;

 . . . .Free to believe but not without asking questions;

 . . . .Free to ask questions but not free to expect all the answers;

. . . .Free to be positive but not free to be a Pollyanna;

. . . .Free to laugh but never at the expense of another;

. . . .Free to be vulnerable but not to force me to be;

. . . .Free to be creative but not to the exclusion of relationships. . . .

. . . .Free to pray but not free to procrastinate;

. . . .Free to be involved but not free to be consumed by busyness;

. . . .Free to face issues but not to lose sight of priorities;

. . . .Free to state your beliefs but not free to harbor anger or bitterness when others' beliefs are different from yours;

. . . .Free to face intimidation but not free to be intimidated;

. . . .Free to dream but not to forget that the dreams come from God;

. . . .Free to fail but not to abandon your dreams because you failed;

. . . .Free to be interdependent but not without first examining and rejecting the options of dependence and independence;

. . . .Free to see living as a privilege, not as a problem.[8]

John 8:36 says if the Son sets you free, you will be free indeed.

> It's a promise we hold on to.
> May the Lord touch your heart
> with his finger of love and leave a
> fingerprint no one can rub off.[9]

12

Soaring Beyond the Power Struggle

FROM FULFILLMENT FOR ONE TO FULFILLMENT FOR BOTH

Grow old along with me. The best is yet to be.

ROBERT BROWNING

Not long ago we spent some quiet moments together sharing a cup of coffee and looking at our wedding pictures. Sixteen years ago, August 7, we committed ourselves to each other for better or worse. It was a holy moment but only one of many. There have been times of standing in the early-morning shadows, arms around one another, silently watching the wonder of sleeping children. There have been the surprises, the friends, the ordination into the ministry, the graduations, the joys, and there have been the seasons of tears. We have worked toward common goals, we have struggled together, and we have laughed in unison. We have been blessed.

But who is that young couple pictured in that wedding album? We barely remember them. Their faces are smooth, their smiles slightly self-conscious, and their love for each other obvious. No wonder our parents offered so many prayers on our behalf. We look so young and so naive. We thought we knew what love and marriage and commitment was all about.

Now, as our eyes meet, we see wrinkles here and there—around the eyes, the mouths, the foreheads. Dave's hairline has receded slightly. My hair has streaks of gray. Yes, we look older than we did, but somehow more interesting.

We've grown so much more comfortable with each other. We not only love being loved now, but over the years we've come to understand more of what it means to love. We not only like being served, we're in the process of learning how to serve. No longer do we view one another as an extension of ourselves or as a "possession" to be owned. Now we are in awe of the separate person with whom we have the privilege of growing.

The competing has ended. Now we see life as a double win or a double lose. No longer are we terrified of losing our individual identities because of our marriage. These days we're rather excited about the people we've become as a result of our relationship. We've stopped trying to control each other and are attempting to free each other to be all God wants us to be. Christ is central to our relationship now, rather than an addition to it. He acts as the glue that holds us together and has corrected our misunderstanding of submission. Mutual submission is now a privilege.

No longer is sex a duty to be performed. It has become a pleasure to be enjoyed. No longer is conflict a thing to be avoided. It has become a tool for widening our perspectives. Listening has become much more important, for it is now a wonderful means of getting to know each other as best friends would. Communication is not just head talk— it is balanced with the heart talk now. It is honest affirmation rather than flattery. Differences are much more tolerable, and we welcome them as friends. Oh, there are times when we wonder where in the world the other is coming from, but our differences have taught us so much about ourselves and each other.

A clear understanding of how much we have been forgiven by our Lord allows us to forgive more easily. We're aware that we're not always ideal mates, but as the Holy Spirit is allowed to operate freely in us, we no longer love power. We've opened the channels through which the power of love becomes evident. No longer is just one of us fulfilled. Now we are both experiencing fulfillment.

We're in process. Some days we thrill each other. Other days we disappoint ourselves and each other. There are laughter and tears. Sometimes we're controlled and other times we're out of control. There are loving moments and indifferent moments. Sometimes we welcome change and other times we're threatened by it. Sometimes we're polite and sometimes we're rude. Being in love means having to say you're sorry.

As a result of these sixteen challenging years we're more in love, more committed, more honest, and more dependent on our Savior. Along with the Velveteen Rabbit, we've become "Real."

"What is REAL?" asked the Rabbit one day. . . . "Does it mean having things that buzz inside you and a stick-out handle?"

"Real isn't how you are made," said the Skin Horse. "It's a thing that happens to you. When a child loves you for a long, long time, not just to play with, but REALLY loves you, then you become Real."

"Does it hurt?" asked the Rabbit.

"Sometimes," said the Skin Horse, for he was

always truthful. "When you are Real you don't mind being hurt."

"Does it happen all at once like being wound up," he asked, "or bit by bit?"

"It doesn't happen all at once," said the Skin Horse. "You become. It takes a long time. That's why it doesn't often happen to people who break easily, or who have sharp edges, or who have to be carefully kept. Generally, by the time you are Real, most of your hair has been loved off, and your eyes drop out and you get loose in the joints and very shabby. But these things don't matter at all, because once you are Real you can't be ugly, except to people who don't understand."

"I suppose *you* are Real?" said the Rabbit . . . The Skin Horse only smiled.

"The Boy's Uncle made me Real," he said. "That was a great many years ago; but once you are Real you can't become unreal again. It lasts for always."[1]

We'll take each other's wrinkles. You see, we're becoming REAL. God's love and our mutual love for each other is transforming us. It's as if we're angels with only one wing. We soar by embracing each other, for Christ's sake. Separately we're interesting but somehow together we're better than either of us is alone. Love is transforming us—not into one another's image but into Christ's image. We wouldn't go back sixteen years for anything. We like becoming Real.

SOURCE NOTES

Preface

1. Inspiration from Luciano De Crescenzo.

Chapter 2 The Misuse of Power

1. John Sterner, *How to Become Super-Spiritual: Or Kill Yourself Trying* (Nashville: Abingdon Press, 1982), p. 44.
2. Rudolph Driekers, *The Challenge of Marriage* (New York: Hawthorn Books, 1949).
3. Mike Mason, *The Mystery of Marriage* (Portland, Oregon: Multnomah Press, 1985), p. 138.

Chapter 3 Making Your Marriage Come Alive

1. Dorothy Corkille Briggs, *Embracing Life: Growing Through Love and Loss* (New York: Doubleday, 1985), p. 69.
2. James H. Olthuis, *I Pledge You My Troth: A Christian View of Marriage, Family, Friendship* (New York: Harper & Row, Publishers, 1975), pp. 9, 10.
3. Elaine Stedman, *A Woman's Worth* (Waco, Texas: Word Books, 1976).

Chapter 4 How to Get Over the Need to Change Your Mate

1. Rose De Wolf, *How to Raise Your Man* (New York: Franklin Watts, 1983), p. 156.
2. Leo Buscaglia, Ph.D., *Loving Each Other* (New York: Fawcett Columbine, 1984), pp. 197, 198.
3. Leo Buscaglia, Ph.D., *Love* (New York: Fawcett Crest, 1986), p. 94.
4. Anne Ortlund, *Building a Great Marriage* (Old Tappan, New Jersey: Fleming H. Revell Company, 1985), p. 23.

Chapter 5 How to Bring Out the Best in Both of You

1. David Viscott, M.D., *How to Live with Another Person* (New York: Arbor House, 1974), p. 19.
2. Rose De Wolf, *How to Raise Your Man* (New York: Franklin Watts, 1983), p. 158.
3. Ruth Harmes Calkin, *Lord, Could You Hurry a Little?* (Wheaton, Illinois: Tyndale House Publishers, 1984), p. 102.
4. Dr. Robert H. Schuller, *Be Happy You Are Loved* (Nashville: Thomas Nelson, 1986), p. 67.
5. Ibid., p. 44.

Chapter 6   Adding Sparkle to Your Marriage

1. Dr. David Viscott, M.D., *How to Live with Another Person*, (New York: Arbor House, 1974), p. 148.
2. Source unknown.
3. "New Woman Tidbits," *New Woman Magazine* (August, 1986), p. 127.
4. Kathy Bence, "A Super Guide to Marriage," *Today's Christian Woman* (September/October, 1984), p. 65.
5. Source unknown.
6. Charlie and Martha Shedd, *Celebration in the Bedroom* (Waco, Texas: Word Books, 1979), p. 57.
7. Dr. and Mrs. David Congo
   Free to Soar Ministries
   P.O. Box 4271
   Mission Viejo, CA 92690-2271
8. Silver Donald Cameron, "The Committed Male: Who, What and Where He Is," *New Woman Magazine* (February, 1987), p. 40.

Chapter 7   Do I Dare to Be Real?

1. Richard Bosch is a Washington television producer who was divorced at age twenty-three. He was quoted in the *Orange County (California) Register* on January 26, 1987.
2. Rose De Wolf, *How to Raise Your Man* (New York: Franklin Watts, 1983), p. 91.
3. Leo Buscaglia, Ph.D. *Love* (New York: Fawcett Crest, 1972), p. 191.
4. Anne Ortlund, *Building a Great Marriage* (Old Tappan, New Jersey: Fleming H. Revell Company, 1985), p. 70.
5. Dr. Robert Anthony, *The Ultimate Secrets of Total Self-Confidence* (New York: Berkeley Books, 1979), pp. 180, 181.
6. Dr. Robert O. Blood, *Marriage: Second Edition* (New York: The Free Press, 1969), p. 204.
7. Paul W. Swets, *The Art of Talking So People Will Listen* (Englewood Cliffs, New Jersey: Prentice-Hall, Inc., 1983), p. 39.
8. John Gottman, *A Couple's Guide to Communication* (Champaign, Illinois: Research Press, 1977), p. 19.
9. Dr. David Seamands, *Reflections in Clergy Couples in Crisis* (Carol Stream, Illinois: Leadership Library, Word, 1985), p. 144, 145.
10. Leo Buscaglia, Ph.D., *Loving Each Other* (New York: Fawcett Columbine, 1984), p. 62.

Chapter 8   Does Anybody Care?

1. Dr. Carl Rogers, "Communication: Its Blocking and Facilitation," *ETC: A Review of General Semantics 9*, No. 2 (International Society for General Semantics, 1952).